PICADOR MODERN
CLASSICS

Celebrated, iconic, and indispensable, Joan Didion's first work of nonfiction, Slouching Towards Bethlehem, *is considered a watershed moment in American writing. First published in 1968, the collection was critically praised as one of the "best prose written in this country."*

More than perhaps any other book, this collection by one of the most distinctive prose stylists of our era captures the unique time and place of Joan Didion's focus, exploring subjects such as John Wayne and Howard Hughes, growing up in California and the nature of good and evil in a Death Valley motel room, and, especially, the essence of San Francisco's Haight-Ashbury, the heart of the counterculture. As Joyce Carol Oates remarked: "[Didion] has been an articulate witness to the most stubborn and intractable truths of our time, a memorable voice, partly eulogistic, partly despairing; always in control."

PUBLISHER'S NOTE

For more than twenty years, Picador has been producing beautifully packaged literary fiction and nonfiction books from Manhattan's Flatiron building. Our Modern Classics line pairs iconic books with a design that's both small enough to fit in your pocket and unique enough to stand out on your bookshelf.

PUBLISHER'S NOTE

ABOUT THE AUTHOR

JOAN DIDION is the author of many works of fiction and nonfiction, including *The Year of Magical Thinking*, for which she received the National Book Award. She lives in New York City.

ALSO BY JOAN DIDION

Fiction

Run River

Play It As It Lays

A Book of Common
  Prayer

Democracy

The Last Thing He
  Wanted

Nonfiction

The White Album

Salvador

Miami

After Henry

Political Fictions

Fixed Ideas: America
  Since 9.11

Where I Was From

The Year of Magical
  Thinking

We Tell Ourselves
  Stories in Order to
  Live: Collected
  Nonfiction

SLOUCHING TOWARDS BETHLEHEM

SLOUCHING TOWARDS
BETHLEHEM

essays

JOAN DIDION

PICADOR MODERN CLASSICS

Farrar, Straus and Giroux
New York

picadorusa.com • picadorbookroom.tumblr.com
twitter.com/picadorusa • facebook.com/picadorusa

Picador® is a U.S. registered trademark and is used by Macmillan Publishing Group, LLC, under license from Pan Books Limited.

"The Second Coming" is reprinted with permission of Mr. M. B. Yeats and Macmillan & Co. Ltd. and The Macmillan Company (New York) from *Collected Poems* by William Butler Yeats. Copyright © 1924 by The Macmillan Company, renewed 1952 by Bertha Georgie Yeats.

For book club information, please visit facebook.com/picadorbookclub or email marketing@picadorusa.com.

Designed by Steven Seighman

The Library of Congress has cataloged the Farrar, Straus and Giroux edition as follows:

Didion, Joan.
  Slouching towards Bethlehem.
    p. cm.
  ISBN 978-0-374-26636-3 (hardcover)
  ISBN 978-0-374-52172-1 (trade paperback)
  1. Essays. I. Title.
  PS3554.I33 S55
  814'.5'4   68014916

Picador Modern Classics ISBN 978-1-250-16065-2

Our books may be purchased in bulk for promotional, educational, or business use. Please contact your local bookseller or the Macmillan Corporate and Premium Sales Department at 1-800-221-7945, extension 5442, or by email at MacmillanSpecial Markets@macmillan.com.

First published by Farrar, Straus and Giroux

First Picador Modern Classics Edition: November 2017

10 9 8 7 6 5 4 3 2

For Quintana

Turning and turning in the widening gyre
The falcon cannot hear the falconer;
Things fall apart; the center cannot hold;
Mere anarchy is loosed upon the world,
The blood-dimmed tide is loosed, and every-
    where
The ceremony of innocence is drowned;
The best lack all conviction, while the worst
Are full of passionate intensity.

Surely some revelation is at hand;
Surely the Second Coming is at hand.
The Second Coming! Hardly are those words
    out
When a vast image out of Spiritus Mundi
Troubles my sight: somewhere in the sands of
    the desert
A shape with lion body and the head of a man,
A gaze blank and pitiless as the sun,
Is moving its slow thighs, while all about it
Reel shadows of the indignant desert birds.
The darkness drops again; but now I know
That twenty centuries of stony sleep
Were vexed to nightmare by a rocking cradle,

*And what rough beast, its hour come round
    at last,*
Slouches towards Bethlehem to be born?

W. B. YEATS

I learned courage from Buddha, Jesus, Lincoln, Einstein, and Cary Grant.

MISS PEGGY LEE

CONTENTS

A PREFACE

THIS BOOK IS CALLED *Slouching Towards Bethlehem* because for several years now certain lines from the Yeats poem which appears two pages back have reverberated in my inner ear as if they were surgically implanted there. The widening gyre, the falcon which does not hear the falconer, the gaze blank and pitiless as the sun; those have been my points of reference, the only images against which much of what I was seeing and hearing and thinking seemed to make any pattern. "Slouching Towards Bethlehem" is also the title of one piece in the book, and that piece, which derived from some time spent in the Haight-Ashbury district of San Francisco, was for me both the most imperative of all these pieces to write and the only one that made me despondent after it was printed. It was the first time I had dealt directly and flatly with the evidence of atomization, the proof that things fall apart: I went to San Francisco because I had not been able to work in some months, had been paralyzed by the conviction that writing was an irrelevant act, that the world as I had understood it no longer existed. If I was to work again at all, it would be necessary for me come to terms with disorder. That was why the piece was important to me. And after it was printed I saw that, however directly and flatly I thought I had said it, I had failed to get through to many of the people who read and even liked the piece, failed to suggest that I was talking about something more general than a handful of children wearing mandalas on their foreheads. Disc jockeys telephoned my house and wanted to discuss (on the air) the incidence of "filth" in the Haight-Ashbury, and acquaintances congratulated me on having finished the piece "just in time," because "the whole fad's dead now, *fini, kaput*." I suppose almost everyone who writes is afflicted some of the time by the suspicion that nobody out there is listening, but it seemed to me then (perhaps because the piece was important to me) that I had never gotten a feedback so universally beside the point.

Almost all of the pieces here were written for magazines during 1965, 1966, and 1967, and most of them, to get that question out of the way at the outset, were "my idea." I was asked to go up to the Carmel Valley and report on Joan Baez's school there; I was asked to go to Hawaii; I think I was asked to write about John Wayne; and I was asked for the short essays on "morality," by *The American Scholar*, and on "self-respect," by *Vogue*. Thirteen of the twenty pieces were published in *The Saturday Evening Post*. Quite often people write me from places like Toronto and want to know (demand to know) how I can reconcile my conscience with writing for *The Saturday Evening Post*; the answer is quite simple. The *Post* is extremely receptive to what the writer wants to do, pays enough for him to be able to do it right, and is meticulous about not changing copy. I lose a nicety of inflection now and then to the *Post*, but do not count myself compromised. Of course not all of the pieces in this book have to do, in a "subject" sense, with the general breakup, with things falling apart; that is a large and rather presumptuous notion, and many of these pieces are small and personal. But since I am neither a camera eye nor much given to writing pieces which do not interest me, whatever I do write reflects, sometimes gratuitously, how I feel.

I am not sure what more I could tell you about these pieces. I could tell you that I liked doing some of them more than others, but that all of them were hard for me to do, and took more time than perhaps they were worth; that there is always a point in the writing of a piece when I sit in a room literally papered with false starts and cannot put one word after another and imagine that I have suffered a small stroke, leaving me apparently undamaged but actually aphasic. I was in fact as sick as I have ever been when I was writing "Slouching Towards Bethlehem"; the pain kept me awake at night and so for twenty and twenty-one hours a day I drank gin-and-hot-water to blunt the pain and took Dexedrine to blunt the gin and wrote the piece. (I would like you to believe that I kept working out of some real professionalism, to meet the deadline, but that would not be entirely true; I did have a deadline, but it was also a troubled time, and working did to the trouble what gin did to the pain.) What else is there to tell? I am bad at interviewing people. I avoid situations in which I have to talk to anyone's press agent. (This precludes doing pieces on most actors, a bonus in itself.) I do not like to make telephone calls, and would not like to count the mornings I have sat on some Best Western motel bed somewhere and tried to force myself to put through the call to the assistant district attorney. My only advantage as a reporter is that I am so physically small, so temperamentally unobtrusive, and so neurotically inarticulate that people tend to forget that my presence runs counter to their best interests. And it always does. That is one last thing to remember: *writers are always selling somebody out.*

SLOUCHING TOWARDS
BETHLEHEM

I
LIFE STYLES IN THE
GOLDEN LAND

Some Dreamers of the Golden Dream

THIS IS A STORY about love and death in the golden land, and begins with the country. The San Bernardino Valley lies only an hour east of Los Angeles by the San Bernardino Freeway but is in certain ways an alien place: not the coastal California of the subtropical twilights and the soft westerlies off the Pacific but a harsher California, haunted by the Mojave just beyond the mountains, devastated by the hot dry Santa Ana wind that comes down through the passes at 100 miles an hour and whines through the eucalyptus windbreaks and works on the nerves. October is the bad month for the wind, the month when breathing is difficult and the hills blaze up spontaneously. There has been no rain since April. Every voice seems a scream. It is the season of suicide and divorce and prickly dread, wherever the wind blows.

The Mormons settled this ominous country, and then they abandoned it, but by the time they left the first orange tree had been planted and for the next hundred years the San Bernardino Valley would draw a kind of people who imagined they might live among the talismanic fruit and prosper in the dry air, people who brought with them Midwestern ways of building and cooking and praying and who tried to graft those ways upon the land. The graft took in curious ways. This is the California where it is possible to live and die without ever eating an artichoke, without ever meeting a Catholic or a Jew. This is the California where it is easy to Dial-A-Devotion, but hard to buy a book. This is the country in which a belief in the literal interpretation of Genesis has slipped imperceptibly into a belief in the literal interpretation of *Double Indemnity*, the country of the teased hair and the Capris and the girls for whom all life's promise comes down to a waltz-length white wedding dress and the birth of a Kimberly or a Sherry or a Debbi and a Tijuana divorce and a return to hairdressers' school.

"We were just crazy kids," they say without regret, and look to the future. The future always looks good in the golden land, because no one remembers the past. Here is where the hot wind blows and the old ways do not seem relevant, where the divorce rate is double the national average and where one person in every thirty-eight lives in a trailer. Here is the last stop for all those who come from somewhere else, for all those who drifted away from the cold and the past and the old ways. Here is where they are trying to find a new life style, trying to find it in the only places they know to look: the movies and the newspapers. The case of Lucille Marie Maxwell Miller is a tabloid monument to that new life style.

Imagine Banyan Street first, because Banyan is where it happened. The way to Banyan is to drive west from San Bernardino out Foothill Boulevard, Route 66: past the Santa Fe switching yards, the Forty Winks Motel. Past the motel that is nineteen stucco tepees: "SLEEP IN A WIGWAM— GET MORE FOR YOUR WAMPUM." Past Fontana Drag City and the Fontana Church

of the Nazarene and the Pit Stop A Go-Go;
past Kaiser Steel, through Cucamonga, out
to the Kapu Kai Restaurant-Bar and Coffee
Shop, at the corner of Route 66 and Carnelian Avenue. Up Carnelian Avenue from the
Kapu Kai, which means "Forbidden Seas,"
the subdivision flags whip in the harsh
wind. "HALF-ACRE RANCHES! SNACK BARS!
TRAVERTINE ENTRIES! $95 DOWN." It is the
trail of an intention gone haywire, the flot-
sam of the New California. But after a while
the signs thin out on Carnelian Avenue, and
the houses are no longer the bright pastels
of the Springtime Home owners but the
faded bungalows of the people who grow a
few grapes and keep a few chickens out
here, and then the hill gets steeper and the
road climbs and even the bungalows are few,
and here—desolate, roughly surfaced, lined
with eucalyptus and lemon groves—is Banyan Street.

Like so much of this country, Banyan
suggests something curious and unnatural. The lemon groves are sunken, down a
three- or four-foot retaining wall, so that one
looks directly into their dense foliage, too

lush, unsettlingly glossy, the greenery of nightmare; the fallen eucalyptus bark is too dusty, a place for snakes to breed. The stones look not like natural stones but like the rubble of some unmentioned upheaval. There are smudge pots, and a closed cistern. To one side of Banyan there is the flat valley, and to the other the San Bernardino Mountains, a dark mass looming too high, too fast, nine, ten, eleven thousand feet, right there above the lemon groves. At midnight on Banyan Street there is no light at all, and no sound except the wind in the eucalyptus and a muffled barking of dogs. There may be a kennel somewhere, or the dogs may be coyotes.

Banyan Street was the route Lucille Miller took home from the twenty-four-hour Mayfair Market on the night of October 7, 1964, a night when the moon was dark and the wind was blowing and she was out of milk, and Banyan Street was where, at about 12:30 a.m., her 1964 Volkswagen came to a sudden stop, caught fire, and began to burn. For an hour and fifteen minutes Lucille Miller ran up and down Banyan calling for help, but no cars passed and no help came. At three o'clock that morning, when the fire had been put out and the California Highway Patrol officers were completing their report, Lucille Miller was still sobbing and incoherent, for her husband had been asleep in the Volkswagen. "What will I tell the children, when there's nothing left, nothing left in the casket," she cried to the friend called to comfort her. "How can I tell them there's nothing left?"

In fact there was something left, and a week later it lay in the Draper Mortuary Chapel in a closed bronze coffin blanketed with pink carnations. Some 200 mourners heard Elder Robert E. Denton of the Seventh-Day Adventist Church of Ontario speak of "the temper of fury that has broken out among us." For Gordon Miller, he said, there would be "no more death, no more heartaches, no more misunderstandings." Elder Ansel Bristol mentioned the "peculiar" grief of the hour. Elder Fred Jensen asked "what shall it profit a man, if he shall gain the whole world, and lose his own soul?" A light rain fell, a blessing in a dry season, and a female vocalist sang "Safe in the Arms of Jesus." A tape recording of the service was made for the widow, who was being held without bail in the San Bernardino County Jail on a charge of first-degree murder.

Of course she came from somewhere else, came off the prairie in search of something she had seen in a movie or heard on the radio, for this is a Southern California story. She was born on January 17, 1930, in Winnipeg, Manitoba, the only child of Gordon and Lily Maxwell, both schoolteachers and both dedicated to the Seventh-Day Adventist Church, whose members observe the Sabbath on Saturday, believe in an apocalyptic Second Coming, have a strong missionary tendency, and, if they are strict, do not smoke, drink, eat meat, use makeup, or wear jewelry, including wedding rings. By the time Lucille Maxwell enrolled at Walla Walla College in College Place, Washington, the Adventist school where her parents then taught, she was an eighteen-year-old possessed of unremarkable good looks and remarkable high spirits. "Lucille wanted to see the world," her father would say in retrospect, "and I guess she found out."

The high spirits did not seem to lend themselves to an extended course of study at Walla Walla College, and in the spring of 1949 Lucille Maxwell met and married Gordon ("Cork") Miller, a twenty-four-old graduate of Walla Walla and of the University of Oregon dental school, then stationed at Fort Lewis as a medical officer. "Maybe you could say it was love at first sight," Mr. Maxwell recalls. "Before they were ever formally introduced, he sent Lucille a dozen and a half roses with a card that said even if she didn't come out on a date with him, he hoped she'd find the roses pretty anyway." The Maxwells remember their daughter as a "radiant" bride.

Unhappy marriages so resemble one another that we do not need to know too much about the course of this one. There may or may not have been trouble on Guam, where Cork and Lucille Miller lived while he finished his Army duty. There may or may not have been problems in the small Oregon town where he first set up private practice. There appears to have been some disappointment about their move to California: Cork Miller had told friends that he wanted to become a doctor, that he was unhappy as a dentist and planned to enter the Seventh-Day Adventist College of Medical Evangelists at Loma Linda, a few miles south of San Bernardino. Instead he bought a dental practice in the west end of San Bernardino County, and the family settled there, in a modest house on the kind of street where there are always tricycles and revolving credit and dreams about bigger houses, better streets. That was 1957. By the summer of 1964 they had achieved the bigger house on the better street and the familiar accouterments of a family on its way up: the $30,000 a year, the three children for the Christmas card, the picture window, the family room, the newspaper photographs that showed "Mrs. Gordon Miller, Ontario Heart Fund Chairman. . . ." They were paying the familiar price for it. And they had reached the familiar season of divorce.

It might have been anyone's bad summer, anyone's siege of heat and nerves and migraine and money worries, but this one began particularly early and particularly badly. On April 24 an old friend, Elaine Hayton, died suddenly; Lucille Miller had seen her only the night before. During the month of May, Cork Miller was hospitalized briefly with a bleeding ulcer, and his usual reserve deepened into depression. He told his accountant that he was "sick of looking at open mouths," and threatened suicide. By July 8, the conventional tensions of love and money had reached the conventional impasse in the new house on the acre lot at 8488 Bella Vista, and Lucille Miller filed for divorce. Within a month, however, the Millers seemed reconciled. They saw a marriage counselor. They talked about a fourth child. It seemed that the marriage had reached the traditional truce, the point at which so many resign themselves to cutting both their losses and their hopes.

But the Millers' season of trouble was not

to end that easily. October 7 began as a commonplace enough day, one of those days that sets the teeth on edge with its tedium, its small frustrations. The temperature reached 102° in San Bernardino that afternoon, and the Miller children were home from school because of Teachers' Institute. There was ironing to be dropped off. There was a trip to pick up a prescription for Nembutal, a trip to a self-service dry cleaner. In the early evening, an unpleasant accident with the Volkswagen: Cork Miller hit and killed a German shepherd, and afterward said that his head felt "like it had a Mack truck on it." It was something he often said. As of that evening Cork Miller was $63,479 in debt, including the $29,637 mortgage on the new house, a debt load which seemed oppressive to him. He was a man who wore his responsibilities uneasily, and complained of migraine headaches almost constantly.

He ate alone that night, from a TV tray in the living room. Later the Millers watched John Forsythe and Senta Berger in *See How They Run*, and when the movie

ended, about eleven, Cork Miller suggested
that they go out for milk. He wanted some
hot chocolate. He took a blanket and pillow
from the couch and climbed into the pas-
senger seat of the Volkswagen. Lucille
Miller remembers reaching over to lock his
door as she backed down the driveway. By
the time she left the Mayfair Market, and
long before they reached Banyan Street,
Cork Miller appeared to be asleep.

There is some confusion in Lucille Miller's mind about what happened between
12:30 a.m., when the fire broke out, and
1:50 a.m., when it was reported. She says
that she was driving east on Banyan Street
at about 35 m.p.h. when she felt the Volkswagen pull sharply to the right. The next
thing she knew the car was on the embankment, quite near the edge of the retaining
wall, and flames were shooting up behind
her. She does not remember jumping out.
She does remember prying up a stone with
which she broke the window next to her
husband, and then scrambling down the retaining wall to try to find a stick. "I don't
know how I was going to push him out," she

says. "I just thought if I had a stick, I'd push him out." She could not, and after a while she ran to the intersection of Banyan and Carnelian Avenue. There are no houses at that corner, and almost no traffic. After one car had passed without stopping, Lucille Miller ran back down Banyan toward the burning Volkswagen. She did not stop, but she slowed down, and in the flames she could see her husband. He was, she said, "just black."

At the first house up Sapphire Avenue, half a mile from the Volkswagen, Lucille Miller finally found help. There Mrs. Robert Swenson called the sheriff, and then, at Lucille Miller's request, she called Harold Lance, the Millers' lawyer and their close friend. When Harold Lance arrived he took Lucille Miller home to his wife, Joan. Twice Harold Lance and Lucille Miller returned to Banyan Street and talked to the Highway Patrol officers. A third time Harold Lance returned alone, and when he came back he said to Lucille Miller, "O.K. . . . you don't talk any more."

When Lucille Miller was arrested the

next afternoon, Sandy Slagle was with her. Sandy Slagle was the intense, relentlessly loyal medical student who used to baby-sit for the Millers, and had been living as a member of the family since she graduated from high school in 1959. The Millers took her away from a difficult home situation, and she thinks of Lucille Miller not only as "more or less a mother or a sister" but as "the most wonderful character" she has ever known. On the night of the accident, Sandy Slagle was in her dormitory at Loma Linda University, but Lucille Miller called her early in the morning and asked her to come home. The doctor was there when Sandy Slagle arrived, giving Lucille Miller an injection of Nembutal. "She was crying as she was going under," Sandy Slagle recalls. "Over and over she'd say, 'Sandy, all the hours I spent trying to save him and now what are they trying to *do* to me?'"

At 1:30 that afternoon, Sergeant William Paterson and Detectives Charles Callahan and Joseph Karr of the Central Homicide Division arrived at 8488 Bella Vista. "One of them appeared at the bedroom door," Sandy Slagle remembers, "and said to Lucille, 'You've got ten minutes to get dressed or we'll take you as you are.' She was in her nightgown, you know, so I tried to get her dressed."

Sandy Slagle tells the story now as if by rote, and her eyes do not waver. "So I had her panties and bra on her and they opened the door again, so I got some Capris on her, you know, and a scarf." Her voice drops. "And then they just took her."

The arrest took place just twelve hours after the first report that there had been an accident on Banyan Street, a rapidity which would later prompt Lucille Miller's attorney to say that the entire case was an instance of trying to justify a reckless arrest. Actually what first caused the detectives who arrived on Banyan Street toward dawn that morning to give the accident more than routine attention were certain apparent physical inconsistencies. While Lucille Miller had said that she was driving about 35 m.p.h. when the car swerved to a stop, an examination of the cooling Volkswagen showed that it was in low gear, and that the parking rather than the driving lights were on. The front wheels, moreover, did not seem to be in exactly the position that Lucille Miller's description of the accident would suggest, and the right rear wheel was dug in deep, as if it had been spun in place. It seemed curious to the detectives, too, that a sudden stop from 35 m.p.h.—the same jolt which was presumed to have knocked over a gasoline can in the back seat and somehow started the fire—should have left two milk cartons upright on the back floorboard, and the remains of a Polaroid camera box lying apparently undisturbed on the back seat.

No one, however, could be expected to give a precise account of what did and did not happen in a moment of terror, and none of these inconsistencies seemed in themselves incontrovertible evidence of criminal intent. But they did interest the Sheriff's Office, as did Gordon Miller's apparent unconsciousness at the time of the accident, and the length of time it had taken Lucille Miller to get help. Something, moreover, struck the investigators as wrong about

Harold Lance's attitude when he came back to Banyan Street the third time and found the investigation by no means over. "The way Lance was acting," the prosecuting attorney said later, "they thought maybe they'd hit a nerve."

And so it was that on the morning of October 8, even before the doctor had come to give Lucille Miller an injection to calm her, the San Bernardino County Sheriff's Office was trying to construct another version of what might have happened between 12:30 and 1:50 a.m. The hypothesis they would eventually present was based on the somewhat tortuous premise that Lucille Miller had undertaken a plan which failed: a plan to stop the car on the lonely road, spread gasoline over her presumably drugged husband, and, with a stick on the accelerator, gently "walk" the Volkswagen over the embankment, where it would tumble four feet down the retaining wall into the lemon grove and almost certainly explode. If this happened, Lucille Miller might then have somehow negotiated the two miles up Carnelian to Bella Vista in time to be home when the accident was discovered. This plan went awry, according to the Sheriff's Office hypothesis, when the car would not go over the rise of the embankment. Lucille Miller might have panicked then—after she had killed the engine the third or fourth time, say, out there on the dark road with the gasoline already spread and the dogs baying and the wind blowing and the unspeakable apprehension that a pair of headlights would suddenly light up Banyan Street and expose her there—and set the fire herself.

Although this version accounted for some of the physical evidence—the car in low because it had been started from a dead stop, the parking lights on because she could not do what needed doing without some light, a rear wheel spun in repeated attempts to get the car over the embankment, the milk cartons upright because there had been no sudden stop—it did not seem on its own any more or less credible than Lucille Miller's own story. Moreover, some of the physical evidence did seem to support her story: a nail in a front tire, a nine-pound rock found in the car, presumably the one with which she had broken the window in an attempt to save her husband. Within a few days an autopsy had established that Gordon Miller was alive when he burned, which did not particularly help the State's case, and that he had enough Nembutal and Sandoptal in his blood to put the average person to sleep, which did: on the other hand Gordon Miller habitually took both Nembutal and Fiorinal (a common headache prescription which contains Sandoptal), and had been ill besides.

It was a spotty case, and to make it work at all the State was going to have to find a motive. There was talk of unhappiness, talk of another man. That kind of motive, during the next few weeks, was what they set out to establish. They set out to find it in accountants' ledgers and double-indemnity clauses and motel registers, set out to determine what might move a woman who believed in all the promises of the middle class—a woman who had been chairman of the Heart Fund and who always knew a reasonable little dressmaker and who had come out of the bleak wild of prairie fundamentalism to find what she imagined to be the good life—what should drive such a woman to sit on a street called Bella Vista and look out her new picture window into the empty California sun and calculate how to burn her husband alive in a Volkswagen. They found the wedge they wanted closer at hand than they might have at first expected, for, as testimony would reveal later at the trial, it seemed that in December of 1963 Lucille Miller had begun an affair with the husband of one of her friends, a man whose daughter called her "Auntie Lucille," a man who might have seemed to have the gift for people and money and the good life that Cork Miller so noticeably lacked. The man was Arthwell Hayton, a well-known San Bernardino attorney and at one time a member of the district attorney's staff.

In some ways it was the conventional clandestine affair in a place like San Bernardino, a place where little is bright or graceful, where it is routine to misplace the future and easy to start looking for it in bed. Over the seven weeks that it would take to try Lucille Miller for murder, Assistant District Attorney Don A. Turner and defense attorney Edward P. Foley would between them unfold a curiously predictable story. There were the falsified motel registrations. There were the lunch dates, the afternoon drives in Arthwell Hayton's red Cadillac convertible. There were the interminable discussions of the wronged partners. There were the confidantes ("I knew everything," Sandy Slagle would insist fiercely later. "I knew every time, places, everything") and there were the words remembered from bad magazine stories ("Don't kiss me, it will trigger things," Lucille Miller remembered telling Arthwell Hayton in the parking lot of Harold's Club in Fontana after lunch one day) and there were the notes, the sweet exchanges: "Hi Sweetie Pie! You are my cup of tea!! Happy Birthday—you don't look a day over 29!! Your baby, Arthwell."

And, toward the end, there was the acrimony. It was April 24, 1964, when Arthwell

Hayton's wife, Elaine, died suddenly, and nothing good happened after that. Arthwell Hayton had taken his cruiser, *Captain's Lady*, over to Catalina that weekend; he called home at nine o'clock Friday night, but did not talk to his wife because Lucille Miller answered the telephone and said that Elaine was showering. The next morning the Haytons' daughter found her mother in bed, dead. The newspapers reported the death as accidental, perhaps the result of an allergy to hair spray. When Arthwell Hayton flew home from Catalina that weekend, Lucille Miller met him at the airport, but the finish had already been written.

It was in the breakup that the affair ceased to be in the conventional mode and began to resemble instead the novels of James M. Cain, the movies of the late 1930's, all the dreams in which violence and threats and blackmail are made to seem commonplaces of middle-class life. What was most startling about the case that the State of California was preparing against Lucille Miller was something that had nothing to do with law at all, something that never ap-

peared in the eight-column afternoon headlines but was always there between them:
the revelation that the dream was teaching
the dreamers how to live. Here is Lucille
Miller talking to her lover sometime in the
early summer of 1964, after he had indicated that, on the advice of his minister, he
did not intend to see her any more: "First, I'm
going to go to that dear pastor of yours and
tell him a few things. . . . When I do tell him
that, you won't be in the Redlands Church
anymore. . . . Look, Sonny Boy, if you think
your reputation is going to be ruined, your
life won't be worth two cents." Here is Arthwell Hayton, to Lucille Miller: "I'll go to
Sheriff Frank Bland and tell him some
things that I know about you until you'll
wish you'd never heard of Arthwell Hayton."
For an affair between a Seventh-Day Adventist dentist's wife and a Seventh-Day Adventist personal-injury lawyer, it seems a curious
kind of dialogue.

"Boy, I could get that little boy coming
and going," Lucille Miller later confided to
Erwin Sprengle, a Riverside contractor who
was a business partner of Arthwell Hayton's

and a friend to both the lovers. (Friend or no, on this occasion he happened to have an induction coil attached to his telephone in order to tape Lucille Miller's call.) "And he hasn't got one thing on me that he can prove. I mean, I've got concrete—he has nothing concrete." In the same taped conversation with Erwin Sprengle, Lucille Miller mentioned a tape that she herself had surreptitiously made, months before, in Arthwell Hayton's car.

"I said to him, I said 'Arthwell, I just feel like I'm being used.' . . . He started sucking his thumb and he said 'I love you. . . . This isn't something that happened yesterday. I'd marry you tomorrow if I could. I don't love Elaine.' He'd love to hear that played back, wouldn't he?"

"Yeah," drawled Sprengle's voice on the tape. "That would be just a little incriminating, wouldn't it?"

"Just a *little* incriminating," Lucille Miller agreed. "It really *is*."

Later on the tape, Sprengle asked where Cork Miller was.

"He took the children down to the church."

"You didn't go?"

"No."

"You're naughty."

It was all, moreover, in the name of "love"; everyone involved placed a magical faith in the efficacy of the very word. There was the significance that Lucille Miller saw in Arthwell's saying that he "loved" her, that he did not "love" Elaine. There was Arthwell insisting, later, at the trial, that he had never said it, that he may have "whispered sweet nothings in her ear" (as her defense hinted that he had whispered in many ears), but he did not remember bestowing upon her the special seal, saying the word, declaring "love." There was the summer evening when Lucille Miller and Sandy Slagle followed Arthwell Hayton down to his new boat in its mooring at Newport Beach and untied the lines with Arthwell aboard, Arthwell and a girl with whom he later testified he was drinking hot chocolate and watching television. "I did that on purpose," Lucille

Miller told Erwin Sprengle later, "to save myself from letting my heart do something crazy."

January 11, 1965, was a bright warm day in Southern California, the kind of day when Catalina floats on the Pacific horizon and the air smells of orange blossoms and it is a long way from the bleak and difficult East, a long way from the cold, a long way from the past. A woman in Hollywood staged an all-night sit-in on the hood of her car to prevent repossession by a finance company. A seventy-year-old pensioner drove his station wagon at five miles an hour past three Gardena poker parlors and emptied three pistols and a twelve-gauge shotgun through their windows, wounding twenty-nine people. "Many young women become prostitutes just to have enough money to play cards," he explained in a note. Mrs. Nick Adams said that she was "not surprised" to hear her husband announce his divorce plans on the Les Crane Show, and, farther north, a sixteen-year-old jumped off the Golden Gate Bridge and lived.

And, in the San Bernardino County Courthouse, the Miller trial opened. The crowds were so bad that the glass courtroom doors were shattered in the crush, and from then on identification disks were issued to the first forty-three spectators in line. The line began forming at 6 a.m., and college girls camped at the courthouse all night, with stores of graham crackers and No-Cal.

All they were doing was picking a jury, those first few days, but the sensational nature of the case had already suggested itself. Early in December there had been an abortive first trial, a trial at which no evidence was ever presented because on the day the jury was seated the San Bernardino *Sun-Telegram* ran an "inside" story quoting Assistant District Attorney Don Turner, the prosecutor, as saying, "We are looking into the circumstances of Mrs. Hayton's death. In view of the current trial concerning the death of Dr. Miller, I do not feel I should comment on Mrs. Hayton's death."

It seemed that there had been barbituates in Elaine Hayton's blood, and there had seemed some irregularity about the way she was dressed on that morning when she was found under the covers, dead. Any doubts about the death at the time, however, had never gotten as far as the Sheriff's Office. "I guess somebody didn't want to rock the boat," Turner said later. "These were prominent people."

Although all of that had not been in the *Sun-Telegram*'s story, an immediate mistrial had been declared. Almost as immediately, there had been another development: Arthwell Hayton had asked newspapermen to an 11 a.m. Sunday morning press conference in his office. There had been television cameras, and flash bulbs popping. "As you gentlemen may know," Hayton had said, striking a note of stiff bonhomie, "there are very often women who become amorous toward their doctor or lawyer. This does not mean on the physician's or lawyer's part that there is any romance toward the patient or client."

"Would you deny that you were having

an affair with Mrs. Miller?" a reporter had asked.

"I would deny that there was any romance on my part whatsoever."

It was a distinction he would maintain through all the wearing weeks to come.

So they had come to see Arthwell, these crowds who now milled beneath the dusty palms outside the courthouse, and they had also come to see Lucille, who appeared as a slight, intermittently pretty woman, already pale from lack of sun, a woman who would turn thirty-five before the trial was over and whose tendency toward haggardness was beginning to show, a meticulous woman who insisted, against her lawyer's advice, on coming to court with her hair piled high and lacquered. "I would've been happy if she'd come in with it hanging loose, but Lucille wouldn't do that," her lawyer said. He was Edward P. Foley, a small, emotional Irish Catholic who several times wept in the courtroom. "She has a great honesty, this woman," he added, "but this honesty about her appearance always worked against her."

By the time the trial opened, Lucille

Miller's appearance included maternity clothes, for an official examination on December 18 had revealed that she was then three and a half months pregnant, a fact which made picking a jury even more difficult than usual, for Turner was asking the death penalty. "It's unfortunate but there it is," he would say of the pregnancy to each juror in turn, and finally twelve were seated, seven of them women, the youngest forty-one, an assembly of the very peers—housewives, a machinist, a truck driver, a grocery-store manager, a filing clerk—above whom Lucille Miller had wanted so badly to rise.

That was the sin, more than the adultery, which tended to reinforce the one for which she was being tried. It was implicit in both the defense and the prosecution that Lucille Miller was an erring woman, a woman who perhaps wanted too much. But to the prosecution she was not merely a woman who would want a new house and want to go to parties and run up high telephone bills ($1,152 in ten months), but a woman who would go so far as to murder her husband for his $80,000 in insurance, making it appear an accident in order to collect another $40,000 in double indemnity and straight accident policies. To Turner she was a woman who did not want simply her freedom and a reasonable alimony (she could have had that, the defense contended, by going through with her divorce suit), but wanted everything, a woman motivated by "love and greed." She was a "manipulator." She was a "user of people."

To Edward Foley, on the other hand, she was an impulsive woman who "couldn't control her foolish little heart." Where Turner skirted the pregnancy, Foley dwelt upon it, even calling the dead man's mother down from Washington to testify that her son had told her they were going to have another baby because Lucille felt that it would "do much to weld our home again in the pleasant relations that we used to have." Where the prosecution saw a "calculator," the defense saw a "blabbermouth," and in fact Lucille Miller did emerge as an ingenuous conversationalist. Just as, before her husband's death, she had confided in her friends about her love affair, so she chatted about it after his death, with the arresting sergeant. "Of course Cork lived with it for years, you know," her voice was heard to tell Sergeant Paterson on a tape made the morning after her arrest. "After Elaine died, he pushed the panic button one night and just asked me right out, and that, I think, was when he really—the first time he really faced it." When the sergeant asked why she had agreed to talk to him, against the specific instructions of her lawyers, Lucille Miller said airily, "Oh, I've always been basically quite an honest person. . . . I mean I can put a hat in the cupboard and say it cost ten dollars less, but basically I've always kind of just lived my life the way I wanted to, and if you don't like it you can take off."

The prosecution hinted at men other than Arthwell, and even, over Foley's objections, managed to name one. The defense called Miller suicidal. The prosecution produced experts who said that the Volkswagen fire could not have been accidental. Foley produced witnesses who said that it could have been. Lucille's father, now a junior-high-school teacher in Oregon, quoted Isaiah to reporters: *"Every tongue that shall rise against thee in judgment thou shalt condemn."* "Lucille did wrong, her affair," her mother said judiciously. "With her it was love. But with some I guess it's just passion." There was Debbie, the Millers' fourteen-year-old, testifying in a steady voice about how she and her mother had gone to a supermarket to buy the gasoline can the week before the accident. There was Sandy Slagle, in the courtroom every day, declaring that on at least one occasion Lucille Miller had prevented her husband not only from committing suicide but from committing suicide in such a way that it would appear an accident and ensure the double-indemnity payment. There was Wenche Berg, the pretty twenty-seven-year-old Norwegian governess to Arthwell Hayton's children, testifying that Arthwell had instructed her not to allow Lucille Miller to see or talk to the children.

Two months dragged by, and the headlines never stopped. Southern California's crime reporters were headquartered in San

Bernardino for the duration: Howard Hertel from the *Times*, Jim Bennett and Eddy Jo Bernal from the *Herald-Examiner*. Two months in which the Miller trial was pushed off the *Examiner*'s front page only by the Academy Award nominations and Stan Laurel's death. And finally, on March 2, after Turner had reiterated that it was a case of "love and greed," and Foley had protested that his client was being tried for adultery, the case went to the jury.

They brought in the verdict, guilty of murder in the first degree, at 4:50 p.m. on March 5. "She didn't do it," Debbie Miller cried, jumping up from the spectators' section. "She didn't *do* it." Sandy Slagle collapsed in her seat and began to scream. "Sandy, for God's sake please *don't*," Lucille Miller said in a voice that carried across the courtroom, and Sandy Slagle was momentarily subdued. But as the jurors left the courtroom she screamed again: "You're murderers. . . . Every last one of you is a *murderer*." Sheriff's deputies moved in then, each wearing a string tie that read "1965 SHERIFF'S RODEO," and Lucille Miller's father, that sad-faced junior-high-school teacher who believed in the word of Christ and the dangers of wanting to see the world, blew her a kiss off his fingertips.

The California Institution for Women at Frontera, where Lucille Miller is now, lies down where Euclid Avenue turns into country road, not too many miles from where she once lived and shopped and organized the Heart Fund Ball. Cattle graze across the road, and Rainbirds sprinkle the alfalfa. Frontera has a softball field and tennis courts, and looks as if it might be a California junior college, except that the trees are not yet high enough to conceal the concertina wire around the top of the Cyclone fence. On visitors' day there are big cars in the parking area, big Buicks and Pontiacs that belong to grandparents and sisters and fathers (not many of them belong to husbands), and some of them have bumper stickers that say "SUPPORT YOUR LOCAL POLICE."

A lot of California murderesses live here, a lot of girls who somehow misunderstood the promise. Don Turner put Sandra Garner here (and her husband in the gas chamber at San Quentin) after the 1959 desert killings known to crime reporters as "the soda-pop murders." Carole Tregoff is here, and has been ever since she was convicted of conspiring to murder Dr. Finch's wife in West Covina, which is not too far from San Bernardino. Carole Tregoff is in fact a nurse's aide in the prison hospital, and might have attended Lucille Miller had her baby been born at Frontera; Lucille Miller chose instead to have it outside, and paid for the guard who stood outside the delivery room in St. Bernardine's Hospital. Debbie Miller came to take the baby home from the hospital, in a white dress with pink ribbons, and Debbie was allowed to choose a name. She named the baby Kimi Kai. The children live with Harold and Joan Lance now, because Lucille Miller will probably spend ten years at Frontera. Don Turner waived his original request for the death penalty (it was generally agreed that he had demanded it only, in

Edward Foley's words, "to get anybody with the slightest trace of human kindness in their veins off the jury"), and settled for life imprisonment with the possibility of parole. Lucille Miller does not like it at Frontera, and has had trouble adjusting. "She's going to have to learn humility," Turner says. "She's going to have to use her ability to charm, to manipulate."

The new house is empty now, the house on the street with the sign that says

PRIVATE ROAD
BELLA VISTA
DEAD END

The Millers never did get it landscaped, and weeds grow up around the fieldstone siding. The television aerial has toppled on the roof, and a trash can is stuffed with the debris of family life: a cheap suitcase, a child's game called "Lie Detector." There is a sign on what would have been the lawn, and the sign reads "ESTATE SALE." Edward Foley is trying to get Lucille Miller's case appealed, but there have been delays. "A trial always comes down to a matter of sympathy," Foley says wearily now. "I couldn't create sympathy for her." Everyone is a little weary now, weary and resigned, everyone except Sandy Slagle, whose bitterness is still raw. She lives in an apartment near the medical school in Loma Linda, and studies reports of the case in *True Police Cases* and *Official Detective Stories*. "I'd much rather we not talk about the Hayton business too much," she tells visitors, and she keeps a tape recorder running. "I'd rather talk about Lucille and what a wonderful person she is and how her rights were violated." Harold Lance does not talk to visitors at all. "We don't want to give away what we can sell," he explains pleasantly; an attempt was made to sell Lucille Miller's personal story to *Life*, but *Life* did not want to buy it. In the district attorney's offices they are prosecuting other murders now, and do not see why the Miller trial attracted so much attention. "It wasn't a very interesting murder as murders go," Don Turner says laconically. Elaine Hayton's death is no longer under investigation. "We know everything we want to know," Turner says.

Arthwell Hayton's office is directly below Edward Foley's. Some people around San Bernardino say that Arthwell Hayton suffered; others say that he did not suffer at all. Perhaps he did not, for time past is not believed to have any bearing upon time present or future, out in the golden land where every day the world is born anew. In any case, on October 17, 1965, Arthwell Hayton married again, married his children's pretty governess, Wenche Berg, at a service in the Chapel of the Roses at a retirement village near Riverside. Later the newlyweds were feted at a reception for seventy-five in the dining room of Rose Garden Village. The bridegroom was in black tie, with a white carnation in his buttonhole. The bride wore a long white *peau de soie* dress and carried a shower bouquet of sweetheart roses with stephanotis streamers. A coronet of seed pearls held her illusion veil.

1966

John Wayne: A Love Song

IN THE SUMMER OF 1943 I was eight, and my father and mother and small brother and I were at Peterson Field in Colorado Springs. A hot wind blew through that summer, blew until it seemed that before August broke, all the dust in Kansas would be in Colorado, would have drifted over the tar-paper barracks and the temporary strip and stopped only when it hit Pikes Peak. There was not much to do, a summer like that: there was the day they brought in the first B-29, an event to remember but scarcely a vacation program. There was an Officers' Club, but no swimming pool; all the Officers' Club had of interest was artificial blue rain behind the bar. The rain interested me a good deal, but I could not spend the summer watching it, and so we went, my brother and I, to the movies.

We went three and four afternoons a week, sat on folding chairs in the darkened

Quonset hut which served as a theater, and
it was there, that summer of 1943 while the
hot wind blew outside, that I first saw John
Wayne. Saw the walk, heard the voice.
Heard him tell the girl in a picture called
War of the Wildcats that he would build her
a house, "at the bend in the river where the
cottonwoods grow." As it happened I did
not grow up to be the kind of woman who
is the heroine in a Western, and although
the men I have known have had many virtues and have taken me to live in many places
I have come to love, they have never been
John Wayne, and they have never taken
me to that bend in the river where the cottonwoods grow. Deep in that part of my
heart where the artificial rain forever falls,
that is still the line I wait to hear.

I tell you this neither in a spirit of self-
revelation nor as an exercise in total recall,
but simply to demonstrate that when John
Wayne rode through my childhood, and
perhaps through yours, he determined forever the shape of certain of our dreams. It
did not seem possible that such a man could
fall ill, could carry within him that most

inexplicable and ungovernable of diseases. The rumor struck some obscure anxiety, threw our very childhoods into question. In John Wayne's world, John Wayne was supposed to give the orders. "Let's ride," he said, and "Saddle up." "Forward *ho*," and "A man's gotta do what he's got to do." "Hello, there," he said when he first saw the girl, in a construction camp or on a train or just standing around on the front porch waiting for somebody to ride up through the tall grass. When John Wayne spoke, there was no mistaking his intentions; he had a sexual authority so strong that even a child could perceive it. And in a world we understood early to be characterized by venality and doubt and paralyzing ambiguities, he suggested another world, one which may or may not have existed ever but in any case existed no more: a place where a man could move free, could make his own code and live by it; a world in which, if a man did what he had to do, he could one day take the girl and go riding through the draw and find himself home free, not in a hospital with something going wrong inside, not in a high bed with

the flowers and the drugs and the forced
smiles, but there at the bend in the bright
river, the cottonwoods shimmering in the
early morning sun.

"Hello, there." Where did he come from,
before the tall grass? Even his history
seemed right, for it was no history at all,
nothing to intrude upon the dream. Born
Marion Morrison in Winterset, Iowa, the
son of a druggist. Moved as a child to Lancaster, California, part of the migration to
that promised land sometimes called "the
west coast of Iowa." Not that Lancaster was
the promise fulfilled; Lancaster was a town
on the Mojave where the dust blew through.
But Lancaster was still California, and it
was only a year from there to Glendale,
where desolation had a different flavor:
antimacassars among the orange groves, a
middle-class prelude to Forest Lawn. Imagine Marion Morrison in Glendale. A Boy
Scout, then a student at Glendale High. A
tackle for U.S.C., a Sigma Chi. Summer vacations, a job moving props on the old Fox
lot. There, a meeting with John Ford, one of
the several directors who were to sense that

into this perfect mold might be poured the inarticulate longings of a nation wondering at just what pass the trail had been lost. "Dammit," said Raoul Walsh later, "the son of a bitch looked like a man." And so after a while the boy from Glendale became a star. He did not become an actor, as he has always been careful to point out to interviewers ("How many times do I gotta tell you, I don't act at all, I *re-act*"), but a star, and the star called John Wayne would spend most of the rest of his life with one or another of those directors, out on some forsaken location, in search of the dream.

> *Out where the skies are a trifle bluer*
> *Out where friendship's a little truer*
> *That's where the West begins.*

Nothing very bad could happen in the dream, nothing a man could not face down. But something did. There it was, the rumor, and after a while the headlines. "I licked the Big C," John Wayne announced, as John Wayne would, reducing those outlaw cells to the level of any other outlaws, but even so we all sensed that this would be the one un-predictable confrontation, the one shoot-out Wayne could lose. I have as much trouble as the next person with illusion and reality, and I did not much want to see John Wayne when he must be (or so I thought) having some trouble with it himself, but I did, and it was down in Mexico when he was making the picture his illness had so long delayed, down in the very country of the dream.

It was John Wayne's 165th picture. It was Henry Hathaway's 84th. It was number 34 for Dean Martin, who was working off an old contract to Hal Wallis, for whom it was independent production number 65. It was called *The Sons of Katie Elder*, and it was a Western, and after the three-month de-lay they had finally shot the exteriors up in Durango, and now they were in the waning days of interior shooting at Estudio Churu-busco outside Mexico City, and the sun was hot and the air was clear and it was lunchtime. Out under the pepper trees the boys from the Mexican crew sat around sucking caramels, and down the road some of the technical men sat around a place which served a stuffed lobster and a glass of tequila for one dollar American, but it was inside the cavernous empty commissary where the talent sat around, the reasons for the exercise, all sitting around the big table picking at *huevos con queso* and Carta Blanca beer. Dean Martin, unshaven. Mack Gray, who goes where Martin goes. Bob Good-fried, who was in charge of Paramount publicity and who had flown down to ar-range for a trailer and who had a delicate stomach. "Tea and toast," he warned repeat-edly. "That's the ticket. You can't trust the lettuce." And Henry Hathaway, the direc-tor, who did not seem to be listening to Goodfried. And John Wayne, who did not seem to be listening to anyone.

"This week's gone slow," Dean Martin said, for the third time.

"How can you say that?" Mack Gray de-manded.

"*This . . . week's . . . gone . . . slow,* that's how I can say it."

"You don't mean you want it to end."

"I'll say it right out, Mack, I want it to *end*. Tomorrow night I shave this beard, I head for the airport, I say *adiós amigos!* Bye-bye *muchachos!*"

Henry Hathaway lit a cigar and patted Martin's arm fondly. "Not tomorrow, Dino."

"Henry, what are you planning to add? A World War?"

Hathaway patted Martin's arm again and gazed into the middle distance. At the end of the table someone mentioned a man who, some years before, had tried unsuccessfully to blow up an airplane.

"He's still in jail," Hathaway said suddenly.

"In jail?" Martin was momentarily distracted from the question whether to send his golf clubs back with Bob Goodfried or consign them to Mack Gray. "What's he in jail for if nobody got killed?"

"Attempted murder, Dino," Hathaway said gently. "A felony."

"You mean some guy just *tried* to kill me he'd end up in jail?"

Hathaway removed the cigar from his mouth and looked across the table. "Some guy just tried to kill *me* he wouldn't end up in jail. How about you, Duke?"

Very slowly, the object of Hathaway's query wiped his mouth, pushed back his chair, and stood up. It was the real thing, the authentic article, the move which had climaxed a thousand scenes on 165 flickering frontiers and phantasmagoric battlefields before, and it was about to climax this one, in the commissary at Estudio Churubusco outside Mexico City. "Right," John Wayne drawled. "I'd kill him."

Almost all the cast of *Katie Elder* had gone home, that last week; only the principals were left, Wayne, and Martin, and Earl Holliman, and Michael Anderson, Jr., and Martha Hyer. Martha Hyer was not around much, but every now and then someone referred to her, usually as "the girl." They had all been together nine weeks, six of them in Durango. Mexico City was not quite Durango; wives like to come along to places like Mexico City, like to shop for handbags, go to parties at Merle Oberon Pagliai's, like to look at her paintings. But Durango. The very name hallucinates. Man's country. Out where the West begins. There had been ahuehuete trees in Durango; a waterfall, rattlesnakes. There had been weather, nights so cold that they had postponed one or two exteriors until they could shoot inside at Churubusco. "It was the girl," they explained. "You couldn't keep the girl out in cold like that." Henry Hathaway had cooked in Durango, *gazpacho* and ribs and the steaks that Dean Martin had ordered flown down from the Sands; he had wanted to cook in Mexico City, but the management of the Hotel Bamer refused to let him set up a brick barbecue in his room. "You really missed something, *Durango*," they would say, sometimes joking and sometimes not, until it became a refrain, Eden lost.

But if Mexico City was not Durango, neither was it Beverly Hills. No one else was using Churubusco that week, and there inside the big sound stage that said LOS HIJOS DE KATIE ELDER on the door, there with the pepper trees and the bright sun outside, they could still, for just so long as the picture lasted, maintain a world peculiar to men who like to make Westerns, a world of loyalties and fond raillery, of sentiment and shared cigars, of interminable desultory recollections; campfire talk, its only point to keep a human voice raised against the night, the wind, the rustlings in the brush.

"Stuntman got hit accidentally on a picture of mine once," Hathaway would say between takes of an elaborately choreographed fight scene. "What was his name, married Estelle Taylor, met her down in Arizona."

The circle would close around him, the cigars would be fingered. The delicate art of the staged fight was to be contemplated.

"I only hit one guy in my life," Wayne would say. "Accidentally, I mean. That was Mike Mazurki."

"Some guy. Hey, Duke says he only hit one guy in his life, Mike Mazurki."

"Some choice." Murmurings, assent.

"It wasn't a choice, it was an accident."

"I can believe it."

"You bet."

"Oh boy. Mike Mazurki."

And so it would go. There was Web Overlander, Wayne's makeup man for twenty years, hunched in a blue Windbreaker, passing out sticks of Juicy Fruit. "*Insect* spray," he would say. "Don't tell us about insect spray. We saw insect spray in Africa, all right. Remember Africa?" Or, "*Steamer* clams. Don't tell us about steamer clams. We got our fill of steamer clams all right, on the *Hatari!* appearance tour. Remember Bookbinder's?" There was Ralph Volkie, Wayne's trainer for eleven years, wearing a red baseball cap and carrying around a clipping from Hedda Hopper, a tribute to Wayne. "This Hopper's some lady," he would say again and again. "Not like some of these guys, all they write is sick, sick, sick, how can you call that guy *sick*, when he's got pains, coughs, works all day, *never complains*. That guy's got the best hook since Dempsey, not *sick*."

And there was Wayne himself, fighting through number 165. There was Wayne, in his thirty-three-year-old spurs, his dusty neckerchief, his blue shirt. "You don't have too many worries about what to wear in these things," he said. "You can wear a blue shirt, or, if you're down in Monument Valley, you can wear a yellow shirt." There was Wayne, in a relatively new hat, a hat which made him look curiously like William S. Hart. "I had this old cavalry hat I loved, but I lent it to Sammy Davis. I got it back, it was unwearable. I think they all pushed it down on his head and said *O.K., John Wayne*—you know, a joke."

There was Wayne, working too soon, finishing the picture with a bad cold and a racking cough, so tired by late afternoon that he kept an oxygen inhalator on the set. And still nothing mattered but the Code. "That guy," he muttered of a reporter who had incurred his displeasure. "I admit I'm balding. I admit I got a tire around my middle. What man fifty-seven doesn't? Big news. Anyway, that guy."

He paused, about to expose the heart of

the matter, the root of the distaste, the fracture of the rules that bothered him more than the alleged misquotations, more than the intimation that he was no longer the Ringo Kid. "He comes down, uninvited, but I ask him over anyway. So we're sitting around drinking mescal out of a water jug."

He paused again and looked meaningfully at Hathaway, readying him for the unthinkable denouement. "He had to be *assisted* to his room."

They argued about the virtues of various prizefighters, they argued about the price of J & B in pesos. They argued about dialogue.

"As rough a guy as he is, Henry, I still don't think he'd raffle off his mother's *Bible*."

"I like a shocker, Duke."

They exchanged endless training-table jokes. "You know why they call this memory sauce?" Martin asked, holding up a bowl of chili.

"Why?"

"Because you *remember it in the morning*."

"Hear that, Duke? Hear why they call this memory sauce?"

They delighted one another by blocking

out minute variations in the free-for-all fight which is a set piece in Wayne pictures; motivated or totally gratuitous, the fight sequence has to be in the picture, because they so enjoy making it. "Listen—this'll really be funny. Duke picks up the kid, see, and then it takes both Dino and Earl to throw him out the door—*how's that?*"

They communicated by sharing old jokes; they sealed their camaraderie by making gentle, old-fashioned fun of wives, those civilizers, those tamers. "So Señora Wayne takes it into her head to stay up and have one brandy. So for the rest of the night it's 'Yes, Pilar, you're right, dear. I'm a bully, Pilar, you're right, I'm impossible.'"

"You hear that? Duke says Pilar threw a table at him."

"Hey, Duke, here's something funny. That finger you hurt today, get the Doc to bandage it up, go home tonight, show it to Pilar, tell her she did it when she threw the table. You know, make her think she was really cutting up."

They treated the oldest among them respectfully; they treated the youngest fondly.

"You see that kid?" they said of Michael Anderson, Jr. "What a kid."

"He don't act, it's right from the heart," said Hathaway, patting his heart.

"Hey kid," Martin said. "You're gonna be in my next picture. We'll have the whole thing, no beards. The striped shirts, the girls, the hi-fi, the eye lights."

They ordered Michael Anderson his own chair, with "BIG MIKE" tooled on the back. When it arrived on the set, Hathaway hugged him. "You see that?" Anderson asked Wayne, suddenly too shy to look him in the eye. Wayne gave him the smile, the nod, the final accolade. "I saw it, kid."

On the morning of the day they were to finish *Katie Elder*, Web Overlander showed up not in his Windbreaker but in a blue blazer. "Home, Mama," he said, passing out the last of his Juicy Fruit. "I got on my getaway clothes." But he was subdued. At noon, Henry Hathaway's wife dropped by the commissary to tell him that she might fly

over to Acapulco. "Go ahead," he told her.
"I get through here, all I'm gonna do is take
Seconal to a point just this side of suicide."
They were all subdued. After Mrs. Hathaway left, there were desultory attempts at
reminiscing, but man's country was receding fast; they were already halfway home,
and all they could call up was the 1961 Bel
Air fire, during which Henry Hathaway
had ordered the Los Angeles Fire Department off his property and saved the place
himself by, among other measures, throw-
ing everything flammable into the swimming pool. "Those fire guys might've just
given it up," Wayne said. "Just let it burn."
In fact this was a good story, and one incor-
porating several of their favorite themes, but
a Bel Air story was still not a Durango story.

In the early afternoon they began the last
scene, and although they spent as much
time as possible setting it up, the moment
finally came when there was nothing to do
but shoot it. "Second team out, first team in,
doors closed," the assistant director shouted
one last time. The stand-ins walked off the
set, John Wayne and Martha Hyer walked

on. "All right, boys, *silencio*, this is a picture." They took it twice. Twice the girl offered John Wayne the tattered Bible. Twice John Wayne told her that "there's a lot of places I go where that wouldn't fit in." Everyone was very still. And at 2:30 that Friday afternoon Henry Hathaway turned away from the camera, and in the hush that followed he ground out his cigar in a sand bucket. "O.K.," he said. "That's it."

Since that summer of 1943 I had thought of John Wayne in a number of ways. I had thought of him driving cattle up from Texas, and bringing airplanes in on a single engine, thought of him telling the girl at the Alamo that "Republic is a beautiful word." I had never thought of him having dinner with his family and with me and my husband in an expensive restaurant in Chapultepec Park, but time brings odd mutations, and there we were, one night that last week in Mexico. For a while it was only a nice evening, an evening anywhere.

We had a lot of drinks and I lost the sense that the face across the table was in certain ways more familiar than my husband's.

And then something happened. Suddenly the room seemed suffused with the dream, and I could not think why. Three men appeared out of nowhere, playing guitars. Pilar Wayne leaned slightly forward, and John Wayne lifted his glass almost imperceptibly toward her. "We'll need some Pouilly-Fuissé for the rest of the table," he said, "and some red Bordeaux for the Duke." We all smiled, and drank the Pouilly-Fuissé for the rest of the table and the red Bordeaux for the Duke, and all the while the men with the guitars kept playing, until finally I realized what they were playing, what they had been playing all along: "The Red River Valley" and the theme from *The High and the Mighty*. They did not quite get the beat right, but even now I can hear them, in another country and a long time later, even as I tell you this.

1965

Where the Kissing
Never Stops

OUTSIDE THE MONTEREY COUNTY COURT-HOUSE in Salinas, California, the Downtown Merchants' Christmas decorations glittered in the thin sunlight that makes the winter lettuce grow. Inside, the crowd blinked uneasily in the blinding television lights. The occasion was a meeting of the Monterey County Board of Supervisors, and the issue, on this warm afternoon before Christmas 1965, was whether or not a small school in the Carmel Valley, the Institute for the Study of Nonviolence, owned by Miss Joan Baez, was in violation of Section 32-C of the Monterey County Zoning Code, which prohibits land use "detrimental to the peace, morals, or general welfare of Monterey County." Mrs. Gerald Petkuss, who lived across the road from the school, had put the problem another way. "We wonder what kind of people would go to a school like this," she asked quite early in the controversy. "Why they aren't out working and making money."

Mrs. Petkuss was a plump young matron with an air of bewildered determination, and she came to the rostrum in a strawberry-pink knit dress to say that she had been plagued "by people associated with Miss Baez's school coming up to ask where it was although they knew perfectly *well* where it was—one gentleman I remember had a beard."

"Well I don't *care*," Mrs. Petkuss cried when someone in the front row giggled. "I have three small children, that's a big responsibility, and I don't like to have to worry about . . ." Mrs. Petkuss paused delicately. "About who's around."

The hearing lasted from two until 7:15 p.m., five hours and fifteen minutes of participatory democracy during which it was suggested, on the one hand, that the Monterey County Board of Supervisors was turning our country into Nazi Germany, and, on the other, that the presence of Miss Baez and her fifteen students in the Carmel Valley would lead to "Berkeley-type" demonstrations, demoralize trainees at Fort Ord, paralyze Army convoys using the Carmel Valley road, and send property values plummeting throughout the county. "Frankly, I can't conceive of anyone buying property near such an operation," declared Mrs. Petkuss's husband, who is a veterinarian. Both Dr. and Mrs. Petkuss, the latter near tears, said that they were particularly offended by Miss Baez's presence on her property during weekends. It seemed that she did not always stay inside. She sat out under trees, and walked around the property.

"We don't start until one," someone from the school objected. "Even if we did make noise, which we don't, the Petkusses could sleep until one, I don't see what the problem is."

The Petkusses' lawyer jumped up. "The *problem* is that the Petkusses happen to have a very beautiful swimming pool, they'd like to have guests out on weekends, like to use the pool."

"They'd have to stand up on a table to see the school."

"They will, too," shouted a young woman

who had already indicated her approval of Miss Baez by reading aloud to the supervisors a passage from John Stuart Mill's *On Liberty*. "They'll be out with spyglasses."

"That is *not* true," Mrs. Petkuss keened. "We see the school out of three bedroom windows, out of one living-room window, it's the only direction we can *look*."

Miss Baez sat very still in the front row. She was wearing a long-sleeved navy-blue dress with an Irish lace collar and cuffs, and she kept her hands folded in her lap. She is extraordinary looking, far more so than her photographs suggest, since the camera seems to emphasize an Indian cast to her features and fails to record either the startling fineness and clarity of her bones and eyes or, her most striking characteristic, her absolute directness, her absence of guile. She has a great natural style, and she is what used to be called a lady. "Scum," hissed an old man with a snap-on bow tie who had identified himself as "a veteran of two wars" and who is a regular at such meetings. "*Spaniel.*" He seemed to be referring to the length of Miss Baez's hair, and was trying to get her attention by tapping with his walking stick, but her eyes did not flicker from the rostrum. After a while she got up, and stood until the room was completely quiet. Her opponents sat tensed, ready to spring up and counter whatever defense she was planning to make of her politics, of her school, of beards, of "Berkeley-type" demonstrations and disorder in general.

"Everybody's talking about their forty- and fifty-thousand-dollar houses and their property values going down," she drawled finally, keeping her clear voice low and gazing levelly at the supervisors. "I'd just like to say one thing. I have more than one *hundred* thousand dollars invested in the Carmel Valley, and I'm interested in protecting my property too." The property owner smiled disingenuously at Dr. and Mrs. Petkuss then, and took her seat amid complete silence.

She is an interesting girl, a girl who might have interested Henry James, at about the time he did Verena Tarrant, in *The Bosto-nians*. Joan Baez grew up in the more evan-gelistic thickets of the middle class, the daughter of a Quaker physics teacher, the granddaughter of two Protestant ministers, an English-Scottish Episcopalian on her mother's side, a Mexican Methodist on her father's. She was born on Staten Island, but raised on the edges of the academic community all over the country; until she found Carmel, she did not really come from anywhere. When it was time to go to high school, her father was teaching at Stanford, and so she went to Palo Alto High School, where she taught herself "House of the Ris-ing Sun" on a Sears, Roebuck guitar, tried to achieve a vibrato by tapping her throat with her finger, and made headlines by re-fusing to leave the school during a bomb drill. When it was time to go to college, her father was at M.I.T. and Harvard, and so she went a month to Boston University, dropped out, and for a long while sang in coffee bars around Harvard Square. She did not much like the Harvard Square life ("They just lie in their pads, smoke pot, and do stupid things like that," said the ministers' granddaughter of her acquaintances there), but she did not yet know another.

In the summer of 1959, a friend took her to the first Newport Folk Festival. She arrived in Newport in a Cadillac hearse with "JOAN BAEZ" painted on the side, sang a few songs to 13,000 people, and there it was, the new life. Her first album sold more copies than the work of any other female folksinger in record history. By the end of 1961 Vanguard had released her second album, and her total sales were behind those of only Harry Belafonte, the Kingston Trio, and the Weavers. She had finished her first long tour, had given a concert at Carnegie Hall which was sold out two months in advance, and had turned down $100,000 worth of concert dates because she would work only a few months a year.

She was the right girl at the right time. She had only a small repertory of Child ballads ("What's Joanie still doing with this Mary Hamilton?" Bob Dylan would fret later), never trained her pure soprano and annoyed some purists because she was indifferent to the origins of her material and sang everything "sad." But she rode in with the folk wave just as it was cresting. She could reach an audience in a way that neither the purists nor the more commercial folksingers seemed to be able to do. If her interest was never in the money, neither was it really in the music: she was interested instead in something that went on between her and the audience. "The easiest kind of relationship for me is with ten thousand people," she said. "The hardest is with one."

She did not want, then or ever, to entertain; she wanted to move people, to establish with them some communion of emotion. By the end of 1963 she had found, in the protest movement, something upon which she could focus the emotion. She went into the South. She sang at Negro colleges, and she was always there where the barricade was, Selma, Montgomery, Birmingham. She sang at the Lincoln Memorial after the March on Washington. She told the Internal Revenue Service that she did not intend to pay the sixty percent of her income tax that she calculated went to the defense establishment. She became the voice that meant protest, although she would always maintain a curious distance from the movement's more ambiguous moments. ("I got pretty sick of those Southern marches after a while," she could say later. "All these big entertainers renting little planes and flying down, always about 35,000 people in town.") She had recorded only a handful of albums, but she had seen her face on the cover of *Time*. She was just twenty-two.

Joan Baez was a personality before she was entirely a person, and, like anyone to whom that happens, she is in a sense the hapless victim of what others have seen in her, written about her, wanted her to be and not to be. The roles assigned to her are various, but variations on a single theme. She is the Madonna of the disaffected. She is the pawn of the protest movement. She is the unhappy analysand. She is the singer who would not train her voice, the rebel who drives the Jaguar too fast, the Rima who hides with the birds and the deer. Above all, she is the girl who "feels" things, who has hung on to the freshness and pain of adolescence, the girl ever wounded, ever young. Now, at an age when the wounds begin to heal whether one wants them to or not, Joan Baez rarely leaves the Carmel Valley.

Although all Baez activities tend to take on certain ominous overtones in the collective consciousness of Monterey County, what actually goes on at Miss Baez's Institute for the Study of Nonviolence, which was allowed to continue operating in the Carmel Valley by a three-two vote of the supervisors, is so apparently ingenuous as to disarm even veterans of two wars who wear snap-on bow ties. Four days a week, Miss Baez and her fifteen students meet at the school for lunch: potato salad, Kool-Aid, and hot dogs broiled on a portable barbecue. After lunch they do ballet exercises to Beatles records, and after that they sit around on the bare floor beneath a photomural of Cypress Point and discuss their reading: *Gandhi on Nonviolence*, Louis Fischer's *Life of Mahatma Gandhi*, Jerome

Frank's *Breaking the Thought Barrier*, Thoreau's *On Civil Disobedience*, Krishnamurti's *The First and Last Freedom* and *Think on These Things*, C. Wright Mills's *The Power Elite*, Huxley's *Ends and Means*, and Marshall McLuhan's *Understanding Media*. On the fifth day, they meet as usual but spend the afternoon in total silence, which involves not only not talking but also not reading, not writing, and not smoking. Even on discussion days, this silence is invoked for regular twenty-minute or hour intervals, a regimen described by one student as "invaluable for clearing your mind of personal hangups" and by Miss Baez as "just about the most important thing about the school."

There are no admission requirements, other than that applicants must be at least eighteen years old; admission to each session is granted to the first fifteen who write and ask to come. They come from all over, and they are on the average very young, very earnest, and not very much in touch with the larger scene, less refugees from it than children who do not quite apprehend it. They worry a great deal about "responding to one another with beauty and tenderness," and their response to one another is in fact so tender that an afternoon at the school tends to drift perilously into the never-never. They debate whether or not it was a wise tactic for the Vietnam Day Committee at Berkeley to try to reason with Hell's Angels "on the hip level."

"O.K.," someone argues. "So the Angels just shrug and say 'our thing's violence.' How can the V.D.C. guy answer that?"

They discuss a proposal from Berkeley for an International Nonviolent Army: "The idea is, we go to Vietnam and we go into these villages, and then if they burn them, we burn too."

"It has a beautiful simplicity," someone says.

Most of them are too young to have been around for the memorable events of protest, and the few who have been active tell stories to those who have not, stories which begin "One night at the Scranton Y . . ." or "Recently when we were sitting in at the A.E.C. . . ." and "We had this eleven-year-old on the Canada-to-Cuba march who was at the time corresponding with a Ghandian, and he...." They talk about Allen Ginsberg, "the only one, the only beautiful voice, the only one talking." Ginsberg had suggested that the V.D.C. send women carrying babies and flowers to the Oakland Army Terminal.

"Babies and flowers," a pretty little girl breathes. "But that's so *beautiful*, that's the whole *point*."

"Ginsberg was down here one weekend," recalls a dreamy boy with curly golden hair. "He brought a copy of the *Fuck Songbag*, but we burned it." He giggles. He is holding a clear violet marble up to the window, turning it in the sunlight. "Joan gave it to me," he says. "One night at her house, when we all had a party and gave each other presents. It was like Christmas but it wasn't."

The school itself is an old whitewashed adobe house quite far out among the yellow hills and dusty scrub oaks of the Upper Carmel Valley. Oleanders support a torn wire fence around the school, and there is no sign, no identification at all. The adobe was a one-room county school until 1950; after that it was occupied in turn by the So Help Me Hannah Poison Oak Remedy Laboratory and by a small shotgun-shell manufacturing business, two enterprises which apparently did not present the threat to property values that Miss Baez does. She bought the place in the fall of 1965, after the County Planning Commission told her that zoning prohibited her from running the school in her house, which is on a ten-acre piece a few miles away. Miss Baez is the vice president of the Institute, and its sponsor; the $120 fee paid by each student for each six-week session includes lodging, at an apartment house in Pacific Grove, and does not meet the school's expenses. Miss Baez not only has a $40,000 investment in the school property but is responsible as well for the salary of Ira Sandperl, who is the president of the Institute, the leader of the discussions, and in fact the *eminence gris* of the entire project. "You might think we're starting in a very small way," Ira Sandperl says. "Sometimes the smallest things can change the course of history. Look at the Benedictine order."

In a way it is impossible to talk about Joan Baez without talking about Ira Sandperl. "One of the men on the Planning Commission said I was being led down the primrose path by the lunatic fringe," Miss Baez giggles. "Ira said maybe he's the lunatic and his beard's the fringe." Ira Sandperl is a forty-two-year-old native of St. Louis who has, besides the beard, a shaved head, a large nuclear-disarmament emblem on his corduroy jacket, glittering and slightly messianic eyes, a high cracked laugh and the general look of a man who has, all his life, followed some imperceptibly but fatally askew rainbow. He has spent a good deal of time in pacifist movements around San Francisco, Berkeley, and Palo Alto, and was, at the time he and Miss Baez hit upon the idea of the Institute, working in a Palo Alto bookstore.

Ira Sandperl first met Joan Baez when

she was sixteen and was brought by her father to a Quaker meeting in Palo Alto. "There was something magic, something different about her even then," he recalls. "I remember once she was singing at a meeting where I was speaking. The audience was so responsive that night that I said 'Honey, when you grow up we'll have to be an evangelical team.'" He smiles, and spreads his hands.

The two became close, according to Ira Sandperl, after Miss Baez's father went to live in Paris as a UNESCO advisor. "I was the oldest friend around, so naturally she turned to me." He was with her at the time of the Berkeley demonstrations in the fall of 1964. "We were actually the outside agitators you heard so much about," he says. "Basically we wanted to turn an *un*violent movement into a *non*violent one. Joan was *en*ormously instrumental in pulling the movement out of its slump, although the boys may not admit it now."

A month or so after her appearance at Berkeley, Joan Baez talked to Ira Sandperl about the possibility of tutoring her for a year. "She found herself among politically knowledgeable people," he says, "and while she had strong *feelings*, she didn't know any of the socio-economic-political-historical terms of nonviolence."

"It was all vague," she interrupts, nervously brushing her hair back. "I want it to be less vague."

They decided to make it not a year's private tutorial but a school to go on indefinitely, and enrolled the first students late in the summer of 1965. The Institute aligns itself with no movements ("Some of the kids are just leading us into another long, big, violent mess," Miss Baez says), and there is in fact a marked distrust of most activist organizations. Ira Sandperl, for example, had little use for the V.D.C., because the V.D.C. believed in nonviolence only as a limited tactic, accepted conventional power blocs, and even ran one of its leaders for Congress, which is anathema to Sandperl. "Darling, let me put it this way. In civil rights, now, the President signs a bill, who does he call to witness it? Adam Powell? No. He calls Rustin, Farmer, King, *none* of them in the conventional power structure." He pauses, as if envisioning a day when he and Miss Baez will be called upon to witness the signing of a bill outlawing violence. "I'm not optimistic, darling, but I'm hopeful. There's a difference. I'm hopeful."

The gas heater sputters on and off and Miss Baez watches it, her duffel coat drawn up around her shoulders. "Everybody says I'm politically naïve, and I am," she says after a while. It is something she says frequently to people she does not know. "So are the people running politics, or we wouldn't be in wars, would we."

The door opens and a short middle-aged man wearing handmade sandals walks in. He is Manuel Greenhill, Miss Baez's manager, and although he has been her manager for five years, he has never before visited the Institute, and he has never before met Ira Sandperl.

"At last!" Ira Sandperl cries, jumping up. "The disembodied voice on the telephone is here at last! There *is* a Manny Greenhill!

There *is* an Ira Sandperl! Here I am! Here's the villain!"

It is difficult to arrange to see Joan Baez, at least for anyone not tuned to the underground circuits of the protest movement. The New York company for which she records, Vanguard, will give only Manny Greenhill's number, in Boston. "Try Area Code 415, prefix DA 4, number 4321," Manny Greenhill will rasp. Area Code 415, DA 4-4321 will connect the caller with Kepler's Bookstore in Palo Alto, which is where Ira Sandperl used to work. Someone at the bookstore will take a number, and, after checking with Carmel to see if anyone there cares to hear from the caller, will call back, disclosing a Carmel number. The Carmel number is not, as one might think by now, for Miss Baez, but for an answering service. The service will take a number, and, after some days or weeks, a call may or may not be received from Judy Flynn, Miss Baez's secretary. Miss Flynn says that she will "try to contact" Miss Baez. "I don't see people," says the heart of this curiously improvised web of wrong numbers, disconnected telephones, and unreturned calls. "I lock the gate and hope nobody comes, but they come anyway. Somebody's been telling them where I live."

She lives quietly. She reads, and she talks to the people who have been told where she lives, and occasionally she and Ira Sandperl go to San Francisco, to see friends, to talk about the peace movement. She sees her two sisters and she sees Ira Sandperl. She believes that her days at the Institute talking and listening to Ira Sandperl are bringing her closer to contentment than anything she has done so far. "Certainly than the singing. I used to stand up there and think I'm getting so many thousand dollars, and for what?" She is defensive about her income ("Oh, I have some money from somewhere"), vague about her plans. "There are some things I want to do. I want to try some rock 'n' roll and some classical music. But I'm not going to start worrying about the charts and the sales because then where are you?"

Exactly where it is she wants to be seems an open question, bewildering to her and even more so to her manager. If he is asked what his most celebrated client is doing now and plans to do in the future, Manny Greenhill talks about "lots of plans," "other areas," and "her own choice." Finally he hits upon something: "Listen, she just did a documentary for Canadian television, *Variety* gave it a great review, let me read you."

Manny Greenhill reads. "Let's see. Here *Variety* says '*planned only a twenty-minute interview but when CBC officials in Toronto saw the film they decided to go with a special—*'" He interrupts himself. "That's pretty newsworthy right there. Let's see now. Here they quote her ideas on peace . . . you know those . . . here she says '*every time I go to Hollywood I want to throw up*' . . . let's not get into that . . . here now, '*her impersonations of Ringo Starr and George Harrison were dead-on,*' get that, that's good."

Manny Greenhill is hoping to get Miss Baez to write a book, to be in a movie, and to get around to recording the rock 'n' roll songs. He will not discuss her income, although he will say, at once jaunty and bleak, "but it won't be much *this* year." Miss Baez let him schedule only one concert for 1966 (down from an average of thirty a year), has accepted only one regular club booking in her entire career, and is virtually never on television. "What's she going to do on Andy Williams?" Manny Greenhill shrugs. "One time she sang one of Pat Boone's songs with him," he adds, "which proves she can get along, but still. We don't want her up there with some dance routine behind her." Greenhill keeps an eye on her political appearances, and tries to prevent the use of her name. "We say, if they use her name it's a concert. The point is, if they haven't used her name, then if she doesn't like the looks of it she can get out." He is resigned to the school's cutting into her schedule. "Listen," he says. "I've always encouraged her to be political. I may not be active, but let's say I'm concerned." He squints into the sun. "Let's say maybe I'm just too old."

To encourage Joan Baez to be "political" is really only to encourage Joan Baez to continue "feeling" things, for her politics are still, as she herself said, "all vague." Her approach is instinctive, pragmatic, not too far from that of any League of Women Voters member. "Frankly, I'm down on Communism," is her latest word on that subject. On recent events in the pacifist movement, she has this to say: "Burning draft cards doesn't make sense, and burning themselves makes even less." When she was at Palo Alto High School and refused to leave the building during a bomb drill, she was not motivated by theory; she did it because "it was the practical thing to do, I mean it seemed to me this drill was impractical, all these people thinking they could get into some kind of little shelter and be saved with canned water." She has made appearances for Democratic administrations, and is frequently quoted as saying: "There's never been a good Republican folksinger"; it is scarcely the diction of the new radicalism. Her concert program includes some of her thoughts about "waiting on the eve of destruction," and her thoughts are these:

My life is a crystal teardrop. There are snowflakes falling in the teardrop and little figures trudging around in slow motion. If I were to look into the teardrop for the next million years, I might never find out who the people are, and what they are doing.

Sometimes I get lonesome for a storm. A full-blown storm where everything changes. The sky goes through four days in an hour, the trees wail, little animals skitter in the mud and everything gets dark and goes completely wild. But it's really God—playing music in his favorite cathedral in heaven—shattering stained glass—playing a gigantic organ— thundering on the keys—perfect harmony—perfect joy.

Although Miss Baez does not actually talk this way when she is kept from the typewriter, she does try, perhaps unconsciously, to hang on to the innocence and turbulence and capacity for wonder, however ersatz or shallow, of her own or of anyone's adolescence. This openness, this vulnerability, is of course precisely the reason why she is so able to "come through" to all the young and lonely and inarticulate, to all those who suspect that no one else in the world understands about beauty and hurt and love and brotherhood. Perhaps because she is older now, Miss Baez is sometimes troubled that she means, to a great many of her admirers, everything that is beautiful and true.

"I'm not very happy with my thinking about it," she says. "Sometimes I tell myself, 'Come on, Baez, you're just like everybody else,' but then I'm not happy with that either."

"Not everybody else has the voice," Ira Sandperl interrupts dotingly.

"Oh, it's all right to have the *voice*, the *voice* is all right . . ."

She breaks off and concentrates for a long while on the buckle of her shoe.

So now the girl whose life is a crystal teardrop has her own place, a place where the sun shines and the ambiguities can be set aside a little while longer, a place where everyone can be warm and loving and share confidences. "One day we went around the room and told a little about ourselves," she confides, "and I discovered that *boy*, I'd had it pretty easy." The late afternoon sun streaks the clean wooden floor and the birds sing in the scrub oaks and the beautiful children sit in their coats on the floor and listen to Ira Sandperl.

"Are you a vegetarian, Ira?" someone asks idly.

"Yes. Yes, I am."

"Tell them, Ira," Joan Baez says. "It's nice."

He leans back and looks toward the ceiling. "I was in the Sierra once." He pauses, and Joan Baez smiles approvingly. "I saw this magnificent tree *growing* out of bare rock, *thrusting* itself . . . and I thought *all right, tree,* if you want to live that much, *all right! All right!* O.K.! I won't chop you! I won't eat you! The one thing we all have in common is that we all want to *live!*"

"But what about vegetables," a girl murmurs.

"Well, I realized, of course, that as long as I was in *this flesh* and *this blood* I couldn't be *perfectly* nonviolent."

It is getting late. Fifty cents apiece is collected for the next day's lunch, and someone reads a request from the Monterey County Board of Supervisors that citizens fly American flags to show that "Kooks, Commies, and Cowards do not represent our County," and someone else brings up the Vietnam Day Committee, and a dissident member who had visited Carmel.

"Marv's an honest-to-God nonviolenter," Ira Sandperl declares. "A man of honesty and love."

"He said he's an anarchist," someone interjects doubtfully.

"Right," Ira Sandperl agrees. "Absolutely."

"Would the V.D.C. call Ghandi bourgeois?"

"Oh, they must know better, but they lead such bourgeois lives themselves . . ."

"That's so true," says the dreamy blond boy with the violet marble. "You walk into their office, they're so unfriendly, so unfriendly and cold . . ."

Everyone smiles lovingly at him. By now the sky outside is the color of his marble, but they are all reluctant about gathering up their books and magazines and records, about finding their car keys and ending the day, and by the time they are ready to leave Joan Baez is eating potato salad with her fingers from a bowl in the refrigerator, and everyone stays to share it, just a little while longer where it is warm.

1966

Comrade Laski, C.P.U.S.A.
(M.-L.)

Michael Laski, also known as M. I. Laski, is a relatively obscure young man with deep fervent eyes, a short beard, and a pallor which seems particularly remarkable in Southern California. With his striking appearance and his relentlessly ideological diction, he looks and talks precisely like the popular image of a professional revolutionary, which in fact he is. He was born twenty-six years ago in Brooklyn, moved as a child to Los Angeles, dropped out of U.C.L.A. his sophomore year to organize for the Retail Clerks, and now, as General Secretary of the Central Committee of the Communist Party U.S.A. (Marxist-Leninist), a splinter group of Stalinist-Maoists who divide their energies between Watts and Harlem, he is rigidly committed to an immutable complex of doctrine, including the notions that the traditional American Communist Party is a "revisionist bourgeois clique," that the Progressive Labor Party, the Trotskyites, and "the revisionist clique headed by Gus Hall" prove themselves opportunistic bourgeois lackeys by making their peace appeal not to the "workers" but to the liberal imperialists; and that H. Rap Brown is the tool, if not the conscious agent, of the ruling imperialist class.

Not long ago I spent some time with Michael Laski, down at the Workers' International Bookstore in Watts, the West Coast headquarters of the C.P.U.S.A. (M.-L.). We sat at a kitchen table beneath the hammer-and-sickle flag and the portraits of Marx, Engels, Mao Tse-tung, Lenin, and Stalin (Mao in the favored center position), and we discussed the revolution necessary to bring about the dictatorship of the proletariat. Actually I was interested not in the revolution but in the revolutionary. He had with him a small red book of Mao's poems, and as he talked he squared it on the table, aligned it with the table edge first vertically and then horizontally. To understand who Michael Laski is you must have a feeling for that kind of compulsion. One does not think of him eating, or in bed. He has nothing in common with the passionate personalities who tend to turn up on the New Left. Michael Laski scorns deviation-ist reformers. He believes with Mao that po-litical power grows out of the barrel of a gun, a point he insists upon with blazing and self-defeating candor. His place in the geography of the American Left is, in short, an almost impossibly lonely and quixotic one, unpopular, unpragmatic. He believes that there are "workers" in the United States, and that, when the time comes, they will "arise," not in anarchy but in conscious con-cert, and he also believes that "the ruling class" is self-conscious, and possessed of de-monic powers. He is in all ways an idealist.

As it happens I am comfortable with the Michael Laskis of this world, with those who live outside rather than in, those in whom the sense of dread is so acute that they turn to extreme and doomed commit-ments; I know something about dread my-self, and appreciate the elaborate systems with which some people manage to fill the void, appreciate all the opiates of the people, whether they are as accessible as alcohol and heroin and promiscuity or as hard to come by as faith in God or History.

But of course I did not mention dread to Michael Laski, whose particular opiate is History. I did suggest "depression," did venture that it might have been "depressing" for him to see only a dozen or so faces at his last May Day demonstration, but he told me that depression was an impediment to the revolutionary process, a disease afflicting only those who do not have ideology to sustain them. Michael Laski, you see, did not feel as close to me as I did to him. "I talk to you at all," he said, "only as a calculated risk. Of course your function is to gather information for the intelligence services. Basically you want to conduct the same probe the F.B.I. would carry out if they could put us in a chair." He paused and tapped the small red book with his fingernails. "And yet," he said finally, "there's a definite advantage to me in talking to you. Because of one fact: these interviews provide a public record of my existence."

Still, he was not going to discuss with me

what he called "the underground apparatus"
of the C.P.U.S.A. (M.-L.), any more than he
would tell me how many members consti-
tuted the cadre. "Obviously I'm not going
to give you that kind of information," he
said. "We know as a matter of course that
we'll be outlawed." The Workers' International Bookstore, however, was "an open
facility," and I was free to look around. I
leafed through some of the literature out of
Peking (*Vice-Premier Chen Yi Answers
Questions Put by Correspondents*), Hanoi
(*President Ho Chi Minh Answers President L. B. Johnson*), and Tirana, Albania
(*The Hue and Cry About a Change in Tito's
Policy and the Undeniable Truth*), and I tried
to hum, from a North Vietnamese song
book, "When the Party Needs Us Our
Hearts Are Filled with Hatred." The literature was in the front of the store, along
with a cash register and the kitchen table;
in back, behind a plywood partition, were a
few cots and the press and mimeograph machine on which the Central Committee
prints its "political organ," *People's Voice,* and
its "theoretical organ," *Red Flag.* "There's a

cadre assigned to this facility in order to guarantee the security," Michael Laski said when I mentioned the cots. "They have a small arsenal in back, a couple of shotguns and a number of other items."

So much security may seem curious when one considers what the members of the cadre actually do, which is, aside from selling the *People's Voice* and trying to set up People's Armed Defense Groups, largely a matter of perfecting their own ideology, searching out "errors" and "mistakes" in one another's attitudes. "What we do may seem a waste of time to some people," Michael Laski said suddenly. "Not having any ideology yourself, you might wonder what the Party offers. It offers nothing. It offers thirty or forty years of putting the Party above everything. It offers beatings. Jail. On the high levels, assassination."

But of course that was offering a great deal. The world Michael Laski had constructed for himself was one of labyrinthine intricacy and immaculate clarity, a world made meaningful not only by high purpose but by external and internal threats, intrigues and apparatus, an immutably ordered world in which things mattered. Let me tell you about another day at the Workers' International Bookstore. The Marxist-Leninists had been out selling the *People's Voice*, and now Michael Laski and three other members of the cadre were going over the proceeds, a ceremony as formal as a gathering of the Morgan partners.

"Mr.—*Comrade*—Simmons—what was the total income?" Michael Laski asked.

"Nine dollars and ninety-one cents."

"Over what period of time?"

"Four hours."

"What was the total number of papers sold?"

"Seventy-five."

"And the average per hour?"

"Nineteen."

"The average contribution?"

"Thirteen and a half cents."

"The largest contribution?"

"Sixty cents."

"The smallest?"

"Four cents."

"It was not a very good day, Comrade Simmons. Can you explain?"

"It's always bad the day before welfare and unemployment checks arrive."

"Very good, Comrade Simmons."

You see what the world of Michael Laski is: a minor but perilous triumph of being over nothingness.

1967

7000 Romaine, Los Angeles 38

SEVEN THOUSAND Romaine Street is in that part of Los Angeles familiar to admirers of Raymond Chandler and Dashiell Hammett: the underside of Hollywood, south of Sunset Boulevard, a middle-class slum of "model studios" and warehouses and two-family bungalows. Because Paramount and Columbia and Desilu and the Samuel Goldwyn studios are nearby, many of the people who live around here have some tenuous connection with the motion-picture industry. They once processed fan photographs, say, or knew Jean Harlow's manicurist. 7000 Romaine looks itself like a faded movie exterior, a pastel building with chipped *art moderne* detailing, the windows now either boarded or paned with chicken-wire glass and, at the entrance, among the dusty oleander, a rubber mat that reads WELCOME.

Actually no one is welcome, for 7000

Romaine belongs to Howard Hughes, and the door is locked. That the Hughes "communications center" should lie here in the dull sunlight of Hammett-Chandler country is one of those circumstances that satisfy one's suspicion that life is indeed a scenario, for the Hughes empire has been in our time the only industrial complex in the world—involving, over the years, machinery manufacture, foreign oil-tool subsidiaries, a brewery, two airlines, immense real-estate holdings, a major motion-picture studio, and an electronics and missile operation—run by a man whose *modus operandi* most closely resembles that of a character in *The Big Sleep*.

As it happens, I live not far from 7000 Romaine, and I make a point of driving past it every now and then, I suppose in the same spirit that Arthurian scholars visit the Cornish coast. I am interested in the folklore of Howard Hughes, in the way people react to him, in the terms they use when they talk about him. Let me give you an example. A few weeks ago I lunched with an old friend at the Beverly Hills Hotel. One of the other guests was a well-married woman in her thirties who had once been a Hughes contract starlet, and another was a costume designer who had worked on a lot of Hughes pictures and who still receives a weekly salary from 7000 Romaine, on the understanding that he work for no one else. He has done nothing but cash that weekly check for some years now. They sat there in the sun, the one-time starlet and the sometime costume designer for a man whose public appearances are now somewhat less frequent than those of The Shadow, and they talked about him. They wondered how he was and why he was devoting 1967 to buying up Las Vegas.

"You can't tell me it's like they say, that he bought the Desert Inn just because the high rollers were coming in and they wouldn't let him keep the penthouse," the ex-starlet mused, fingering a diamond as big as the Ritz. "It must be part of some larger mission."

The phrase was exactly right. Anyone who skims the financial press knows that Hughes never has business "transactions," or "negotiations"; he has "missions." His central mission, as *Fortune* once put it in a series of love letters, has always been "to preserve his power as the proprietor of the largest pool of industrial wealth still under the absolute control of a single individual." Nor does Hughes have business "associates"; he has only "adversaries." When the adversaries "appear to be" threatening his absolute control, Hughes "might or might not" take action. It is such phrases as "appear to be" and "might or might not," peculiar to business reportage involving Hughes, that suggested the special mood of a Hughes mission. And here is what the action might or might not be: Hughes might warn, at the critical moment, "You're holding a gun to my head." If there is one thing Hughes dislikes, it is a gun to his head (generally this means a request for an appearance, or a discussion of policy), and at least one president of T.W.A., a company which, as Hughes ran it, bore an operational similarity only to the government of Honduras, departed on this note.

The stories are endless, infinitely familiar, traded by the faithful like baseball cards, fondled until they fray around the edges and blur into the apocryphal. There is the one about the barber, Eddie Alexander, who was paid handsomely to remain on "day and night standby" in case Hughes wanted a haircut. "Just checking, Eddie," Hughes once said when he called Alexander at two in the morning. "Just wanted to see if you were standing by." There was the time Convair wanted to sell Hughes 340 transports and Hughes insisted that, to insure "secrecy," the mission be discussed only between midnight and dawn, by flashlight, in the Palm Springs Municipal Dump. There was the evening when both Hughes and Greg Bautzer, then his lawyer, went incommunicado while, in the conference room of the Chemical Bank in New York, the money men waited to lend T.W.A. $165 million. There they were, $165 million in hand, the men from two of the country's biggest insurance companies and nine of its most powerful banks, all waiting, and it was 7 p.m. of the last day the deal could be made and the bankers found themselves talking by phone not to Hughes, not even to Bautzer, but to Bautzer's wife, the movie star Dana Wynter. "I hope he takes it in pennies," a Wall Street broker said when Hughes, six years later, sold T.W.A. for $546 million, "and drops it on his toes."

Then there are the more recent stories. Howard Hughes is en route to Boston aboard the Super Chief with the Bel Air Patrol riding shotgun. Howard Hughes is in Peter Bent Brigham Hospital. Howard Hughes commandeers the fifth floor of the Boston Ritz. Howard Hughes is or is not buying 37 ½ percent of Columbia Pictures through the Swiss Banque de Paris. Howard Hughes is ill. Howard Hughes is dead. No, Howard Hughes is in Las Vegas. Howard Hughes pays $13 million for the Desert Inn. $15 million for the Sands. Gives the State of Nevada $6 million for a medical school. Negotiates for ranches, Alamo Airways, the North Las Vegas Air Terminal, more ranches, the rest of the Strip. By July of 1967 Howard Hughes is the largest single landholder in Clark County, Nevada. "Howard likes Las Vegas," an acquaintance of Hughes's once explained, "because he likes to be able to find a restaurant open in case he wants a sandwich."

Why do we like those stories so? Why do we tell them over and over? Why have we made a folk hero of a man who is the antithesis of all our official heroes, a haunted millionaire out of the West, trailing a legend of desperation and power and white sneakers? But then we have always done that. Our favorite people and our favorite stories become so not by any inherent virtue, but because they illustrate something deep in the grain, something unadmitted. Shoeless Joe Jackson, Warren Gamaliel Harding, the *Titanic: how the mighty are fallen.* Charles Lindbergh, Scott and Zelda Fitzgerald, Marilyn Monroe: *the beautiful and damned.* And Howard Hughes. That we have made a hero of Howard Hughes tells us something interesting about ourselves, something only dimly remembered, tells us that the secret point of money and power in America is neither the things that money can buy nor power for power's sake (Americans are uneasy with their possessions, guilty about power, all of which is difficult for Europeans to perceive because they are themselves so truly materialistic, so versed in the uses of power), but absolute personal freedom, mobility, privacy. It is the instinct which drove America to the Pacific, all through the nineteenth century, the desire to be able to find a restaurant open in case you want a sandwich, to be a free agent, live by one's own rules.

Of course we do not admit that. The instinct is socially suicidal, and because we recognize that this is so we have developed workable ways of saying one thing and believing quite another. A long time ago, Lionel Trilling pointed out what he called "the fatal separation" between "the ideas of our educated liberal class and the deep places of the imagination." "I mean only," he wrote, "that our educated class has a ready if mild suspiciousness of the profit motive, a belief in progress, science, social legislation, planning and international cooperation. . . . Those beliefs do great credit to those who hold them. Yet it is a comment, if not on our beliefs then on our way of holding them, that not a single first-rate writer has emerged to deal with these ideas, and the emotions that are consonant with them, in a great literary way." Officially we admire men who exemplify those ideas. We admire the Adlai Stevenson character, the rational man, the enlightened man, the man not dependent upon the potentially psychopathic mode of action. Among rich men, we officially admire Paul Mellon, a socially responsible inheritor in the European mold. There has always been that divergence between our official and our unofficial heroes. It is impossible to think of Howard Hughes without seeing the apparently bottomless gulf between what we say we want and what we do want, between what we officially admire and secretly desire, between, in the largest sense, the people we marry and the people we love. In a nation which increasingly appears to prize social virtues, Howard Hughes remains not merely antisocial but grandly, brilliantly, surpassingly, asocial. He is the last private man, the dream we no longer admit.

1967

California Dreaming

EVERY WEEKDAY MORNING at eleven o'clock, just about the time the sun burns the last haze off the Santa Barbara hills, fifteen or twenty men gather in what was once the dining room of a shirt manufacturer's mansion overlooking the Pacific Ocean and begin another session of what they like to call "clarifying the basic issues." The place is the Center for the Study of Democratic Institutions, the current mutation of the Fund for the Republic, and since 1959, when the Fund paid $250,000 for the marble villa and forty-one acres of eucalyptus, a favored retreat for people whom the Center's president, Robert M. Hutchins, deems controversial, stimulating, and, perhaps above all, cooperative, or *our kind.* "If they just want to work on their own stuff," Hutchins has said, "then they ought not to come here. Unless they're willing to come in and work with the group as a group, then this place is not for them."

Those invited to spend time at the Center get an office (there are no living quarters at the Center) and a salary, the size of which is reportedly based on the University of California pay scale. The selection process is usually described as "mysterious," but it always involves "people we know." Paul Hoffman, who was at one time president of the Ford Foundation and then director of the Fund for the Republic, is now the Center's honorary chairman, and his son is there quite a bit, and Robert Hutchins's son-in-law. Rexford Tugwell, one of the New Deal "brain trust," is there ("Why not?" he asked me. "If I weren't here I'd be in a rest home"), and Harvey Wheeler, the co-author of *Fail-Safe*. Occasionally someone might be asked to the Center because he has built-in celebrity value, *e.g.*, Bishop James Pike. "What we are is a group of highly skilled public-relations experts," Harry Ashmore says. Harry Ashmore is a fixture at the Center, and he regards Hutchins—or, as the president of the Center is inflexibly referred to in the presence of outsiders, Dr. Hutchins—as "a natural intellectual resource." What these highly skilled public-relations experts do, besides clarifying the basic issues and giving a lift to Bennett Cerf ("My talk with Paul Hoffman on the Coast gave me a lift I won't forget," Bennett Cerf observed some time ago), is to gather every weekday for a few hours of discussion, usually about one of several broad areas that the Center is concentrating upon at any given time—The City, say, or The Emerging Constitution. Papers are prepared, read, revised, reread, and sometimes finally published. This process is variously described by those who participate in it as "pointing the direction for all of us toward a greater understanding" and "applying human reason to the complex problems of our brand-new world."

I have long been interested in the Center's rhetoric, which has about it the kind of ectoplasmic generality that always makes me sense I am on the track of the real soufflé, the genuine American *kitsch*, and so not long ago I arranged to attend a few sessions in Santa Barbara. It was in no sense time

wasted. The Center is the most perfectly in-
digenous cultural phenomenon since the En-
cyclopaedia Britannica's *Syntopicon*, which
sets forth "The 102 Great Ideas of Western
Man" and which we also owe to Robert, or
Dr., Hutchins. "Don't make the mistake of
taking a chair at the big table," I was warned
sotto voce on my first visit to the Center. "The
talk there is pretty high-powered."

"Is there any evidence that living in a violent age encourages violence?" someone
was asking at the big table.

"That's hard to measure."

"I think it's the Westerns on television."

"I tend [*pause*] to agree."

Every word uttered at the Center is pre-
served on tape, and not only colleges and
libraries but thousands of individuals receive Center tapes and pamphlets. Among
the bestselling pamphlets have been A. A.
Berle, Jr.'s *Economic Power and the Free Society*, Clark Kerr's *Unions and Union Leaders
of Their Own Choosing*, Donald Michael's
Cybernation: The Silent Conquest, and Harrison Brown's *Community of Fear*. Seventy-
five thousand people a year then write fan

letters to the Center, confirming the staff in its conviction that everything said around the place mystically improves the national, and in fact the international, weal. From a Colorado country-day-school teacher: "I use the Center's various papers in my U.S. history-current events course. It seems to me that there is no institution in the U.S. today engaged in more valuable and first-rate work than the Center." From a California mother: "Now my fifteen-year-old daughter has discovered your publications. This delights me as she is one of those regular teenagers. But when she curls up to read, it is with your booklets."

The notion that providing useful papers for eighth-grade current-events classes and reading for regular teenagers might not be at all times compatible with establishing "a true intellectual community" (another Hutchins aim) would be considered, at the Center, a downbeat and undemocratic cavil. "People are entitled to learn what we're thinking," someone there told me. The place is in fact avidly anti-intellectual, the deprecatory use of words like "egghead" and "ivory tower" reaching heights matched only in a country-club locker room. Hutchins takes pains to explain that by "an intellectual community" he does not mean a community "whose members regard themselves as 'intellectuals.'" Harry Ashmore frets particularly that "men of affairs" may fail to perceive the Center's "practical utility." Hutchins likes to quote Adlai Stevenson on this point: "The Center can be thought of as a kind of national insurance plan, a way of making certain that we will deserve better and better."

Although one suspects that this pragmatic Couéism as a mode of thought comes pretty naturally to most of the staff at the Center, it is also vital to the place's survival. In 1959 the Fund for the Republic bequeathed to the Center the $4 million left of its original $15 million Ford Foundation grant, but that is long gone, and because there was never any question of more Ford money, the Center must pay its own way. Its own way costs about a million dollars a year. Some twelve thousand contributors provide the million a year, and it helps if they can think of a gift to the Center not as a gift to support some visionaries who never met a payroll but "as an investment [tax-exempt] in the preservation of our free way of life." It helps, too, to present the donor with a fairly broad-stroke picture of how the Center is besieged by the forces of darkness, and in this effort the Center has had an invaluable, if unintentional, ally in the Santa Barbara John Birch Society. "You can't let the fascists drive them out of town," I was advised by an admirer of the Center.

Actually, even without the Birch Society as a foil, Hutchins has evolved the $E=mc^2$ of all fund-raising formulae. The Center is supported on the same principle as a vanity press. People who are in a position to contribute large sums of money are encouraged to participate in clarifying the basic issues. Dinah Shore, a founding member, is invited up to discuss civil rights with Bayard Rustin. Steve Allen talks over "Ideology and Intervention" with Senator Fulbright and Arnold Toynbee, and Kirk Douglas, a founding member, speaks his piece on "The Arts in a Democratic Society." Paul Newman, in the role of "concerned citizen," is on hand to discuss "The University in America" with Dr. Hutchins, Supreme Court Justice William O. Douglas, Arnold Grant, Rosemary Park, and another concerned citizen, Jack Lemmon. "Apropos of absolutely nothing," Mr. Lemmon says, pulling on a pipe, "just for my own amazement—I don't *know*, but I *want* to know—" At this juncture he wants to know about student unrest, and, at another, he worries that government contracts will corrupt "pure research."

"You mean maybe they get a grant to develop some new kind of *plastic*," Mr. Newman muses, and Mr. Lemmon picks up the cue: "What happens then to the humanities?"

Everyone goes home flattered, and the Center prevails. Well, why not? One morning I was talking with the wife of a big contributor as we waited on the terrace for one of the Center's ready-mixed martinis and a few moments' chat with Dr. Hutchins. "These sessions are way over my head," she confided, "but I go out floating on air."

1967

Marrying Absurd

TO BE MARRIED in Las Vegas, Clark County, Nevada, a bride must swear that she is eighteen or has parental permission and a bridegroom that he is twenty-one or has parental permission. Someone must put up five dollars for the license. (On Sundays and holidays, fifteen dollars. The Clark County Courthouse issues marriage licenses at any time of the day or night except between noon and one in the afternoon, between eight and nine in the evening, and between four and five in the morning.) Nothing else is required. The State of Nevada, alone among these United States, demands neither a premarital blood test nor a waiting period before or after the issuance of a marriage license. Driving in across the Mojave from Los Angeles, one sees the signs way out on the desert, looming up from that moonscape of rattlesnakes and mesquite, even before the Las Vegas lights appear like a

mirage on the horizon: "GETTING MAR-
RIED? Free License Information First Strip
Exit." Perhaps the Las Vegas wedding industry achieved its peak operational effi-
ciency between 9:00 p.m. and midnight of
August 26, 1965, an otherwise unremarkable Thursday which happened to be, by
Presidential order, the last day on which
anyone could improve his draft status
merely by getting married. One hundred
and seventy-one couples were pronounced
man and wife in the name of Clark County
and the State of Nevada that night, sixty-
seven of them by a single justice of the peace,
Mr. James A. Brennan. Mr. Brennan did one
wedding at the Dunes and the other sixty-six
in his office, and charged each couple eight
dollars. One bride lent her veil to six others.
"I got it down from five to three minutes,"
Mr. Brennan said later of his feat. "I could've
married them *en masse*, but they're people,
not cattle. People expect more when they
get married."

What people who get married in Las Vegas actually do expect—what, in the largest sense, their "expectations" are—strikes

one as a curious and self-contradictory business. Las Vegas is the most extreme and allegorical of American settlements, bizarre and beautiful in its venality and in its devotion to immediate gratification, a place the tone of which is set by mobsters and call girls and ladies' room attendants with amyl nitrite poppers in their uniform pockets. Almost everyone notes that there is no "time" in Las Vegas, no night and no day and no past and no future (no Las Vegas casino, however, has taken the obliteration of the ordinary time sense quite so far as Harold's Club in Reno, which for a while issued, at odd intervals in the day and night, mimeographed "bulletins" carrying news from the world outside); neither is there any logical sense of where one is. One is standing on a highway in the middle of a vast hostile desert looking at an eighty-foot sign which blinks "STARDUST" or "CAESAR'S PALACE." Yes, but what does that explain? This geographical implausibility reinforces the sense that what happens there has no connection with "real" life; Nevada cities like Reno and Carson are ranch towns, Western towns, places behind which there is some historical imperative. But Las Vegas seems to exist only in the eye of the beholder. All of which makes it an extraordinarily stimulating and interesting place, but an odd one in which to want to wear a candlelight satin Priscilla of Boston wedding dress with Chantilly lace insets, tapered sleeves and a detachable modified train.

And yet the Las Vegas wedding business seems to appeal to precisely that impulse. "Sincere and Dignified Since 1954," one wedding chapel advertises. There are nineteen such wedding chapels in Las Vegas, intensely competitive, each offering better, faster, and, by implication, more sincere services than the next: Our Photos Best Anywhere, Your Wedding on A Phonograph Record, Candlelight with Your Ceremony, Honeymoon Accommodations, Free Transportation from Your Motel to Courthouse to Chapel and Return to Motel, Religious or Civil Ceremonies, Dressing Rooms, Flowers, Rings, Announcements, Witnesses Available, and Ample Parking. All of these services, like most others in Las

Vegas (sauna baths, payroll-check cashing, chinchilla coats for sale or rent) are offered twenty-four hours a day, seven days a week, presumably on the premise that marriage, like craps, is a game to be played when the table seems hot.

But what strikes one most about the Strip chapels, with their wishing wells and stained-glass paper windows and their artificial bouvardia, is that so much of their business is by no means a matter of simple convenience, of late-night liaisons between show girls and baby Crosbys. Of course there is some of that. (One night about eleven o'clock in Las Vegas I watched a bride in an orange minidress and masses of flame-colored hair stumble from a Strip chapel on the arm of her bridegroom, who looked the part of the expendable nephew in movies like *Miami Syndicate*. "I gotta get the kids," the bride whimpered. "I gotta pick up the sitter, I gotta get to the midnight show." "What you gotta get," the bridegroom said, opening the door of a Cadillac Coupe de Ville and watching her crumple on the seat, "is sober.") But Las Vegas seems to offer something other than "convenience"; it is merchandising "niceness," the facsimile of proper ritual, to children who do not know how else to find it, how to make the arrangements, how to do it "right." All day and evening long on the Strip, one sees actual wedding parties, waiting under the harsh lights at a crosswalk, standing uneasily in the parking lot of the Frontier while the photographer hired by The Little Church of the West ("Wedding Place of the Stars") certifies the occasion, takes the picture: the bride in a veil and white satin pumps, the bridegroom usually in a white dinner jacket, and even an attendant or two, a sister or a best friend in hot-pink *peau de soie*, a flirtation veil, a carnation nosegay. "When I Fall in Love It Will Be Forever," the organist plays, and then a few bars of Lohengrin. The mother cries; the stepfather, awkward in his role, invites the chapel hostess to join them for a drink at the Sands. The hostess declines with a professional smile; she has already transferred her interest to the group waiting outside. One bride out, another in, and again the sign goes up on the chapel door: "One moment please—Wedding."

I sat next to one such wedding party in a Strip restaurant the last time I was in Las Vegas. The marriage had just taken place; the bride still wore her dress, the mother her corsage. A bored waiter poured out a few swallows of pink champagne ("on the house") for everyone but the bride, who was too young to be served. "You'll need something with more kick than that," the bride's father said with heavy jocularity to his new son-in-law; the ritual jokes about the wedding night had a certain Panglossian character, since the bride was clearly several months pregnant. Another round of pink champagne, this time not on the house, and the bride began to cry. "It was just as nice," she sobbed, "as I hoped and dreamed it would be."

1967

Slouching Towards Bethlehem

THE CENTER WAS not holding. It was a country of bankruptcy notices and public-auction announcements and commonplace reports of casual killings and misplaced children and abandoned homes and vandals who misspelled even the four-letter words they scrawled. It was a country in which families routinely disappeared, trailing bad checks and repossession papers. Adolescents drifted from city to torn city, sloughing off both the past and the future as snakes shed their skins, children who were never taught and would never now learn the games that had held the society together. People were missing. Children were missing. Parents were missing. Those left behind filed desultory missing-persons reports, then moved on themselves.

It was not a country in open revolution. It was not a country under enemy siege. It was the United States of America in the cold late spring of 1967, and the market was steady and the G.N.P. high and a great many articulate people seemed to have a sense of high social purpose and it might have been a spring of brave hopes and national promise, but it was not, and more and more people had the uneasy apprehension that it was not. All that seemed clear was that at some point we had aborted ourselves and butchered the job, and because nothing else seemed so relevant I decided to go to San Francisco. San Francisco was where the social hemorrhaging was showing up. San Francisco was where the missing children were gathering and calling themselves "hippies." When I first went to San Francisco in that cold late spring of 1967 I did not even know what I wanted to find out, and so I just stayed around awhile, and made a few friends.

A sign on Haight Street, San Francisco:

> *Last Easter Day*
> *My Christopher Robin wandered away.*

He called April 10th
But he hasn't called since
He said he was coming home
But he hasn't shown.

If you see him on Haight
Please tell him not to wait
I need him now
I don't care how
If he needs the bread
I'll send it ahead.

If there's hope
Please write me a note
If he's still there
Tell him how much I care
Where he's at I need to know
For I really love him so!

> *Deeply,*
> *Marla*

Marla Pence
12702 NE. Multnomah
Portland, Ore. 97230
503/252-2720.

I am looking for somebody called Dead-eye and I hear he is on the Street this afternoon doing a little business, so I keep an eye out for him and pretend to read the signs in the Psychedelic Shop on Haight Street when a kid, sixteen, seventeen, comes in and sits on the floor beside me.

"What are you looking for," he says.

I say nothing much.

"I been out of my mind for three days," he says. He tells me he's been shooting crystal, which I already pretty much know because he does not bother to keep his sleeves rolled down over the needle tracks. He came up from Los Angeles some number of weeks ago, he doesn't remember what number, and now he'll take off for New York, if he can find a ride. I show him a sign offering a ride to Chicago. He wonders where Chicago is. I ask where he comes from. "Here," he says. I mean before here. "San Jose, Chula Vista, I dunno. My mother's in Chula Vista."

A few days later I run into him in Golden Gate Park when the Grateful Dead are playing. I ask if he found a ride to New York. "I hear New York's a bummer," he says.

Deadeye never showed up that day on the Street, and somebody says maybe I can find him at his place. It is three o'clock and Deadeye is in bed. Somebody else is asleep on the living-room couch, and a girl is sleeping on the floor beneath a poster of Allen Ginsberg, and there are a couple of girls in pajamas making instant coffee. One of the girls introduces me to the friend on the couch, who extends one arm but does not get up because he is naked. Deadeye and I have a mutual acquaintance, but he does not mention his name in front of the others. "The man you talked to," he says, or "that man I was referring to earlier." The man is a cop.

The room is overheated and the girl on the floor is sick. Deadeye says she has been sleeping for twenty-four hours now. "Lemme ask you something," he says. "You want some grass?" I say I have to be moving on. "You want it," Deadeye says, "it's yours." Deadeye used to be an Angel around Los Angeles but that was a few years ago. "Right now," he says, "I'm trying to set up this groovy religious group—'Teenage Evangelism.'"

Don and Max want to go out to dinner but Don is only eating macrobiotic so we end up in Japantown again. Max is telling me how he lives free of all the old middle-class Freudian hang-ups. "I've had this old lady for a couple of months now, maybe she makes something special for my dinner and I come in three days late and tell her I've been balling some other chick, well, maybe she shouts a little but then I say 'That's me, baby,' and she laughs and says 'That's you, Max.'" Max says it works both ways. "I mean if she comes in and tells me she wants to ball Don, maybe, I say 'O.K., baby, it's your trip.'"

Max sees his life as a triumph over

"don'ts." Among the don'ts he had done before he was twenty-one were peyote, alcohol, mescaline, and Methedrine. He was on a Meth trip for three years in New York and Tangier before he found acid. He first tried peyote when he was in an Arkansas boys' school and got down to the Gulf and met "an Indian kid who was doing a don't. Then every weekend I could get loose I'd hitchhike seven hundred miles to Brownsville, Texas, so I could cop peyote. Peyote went for thirty cents a button down in Brownsville on the street." Max dropped in and out of most of the schools and fashionable clinics in the eastern half of America, his standard technique for dealing with boredom being to leave. Example: Max was in a hospital in New York and "the night nurse was a groovy spade, and in the afternoon for therapy there was a chick from Israel who was interesting, but there was nothing much to do in the morning, so I left."

We drink some more green tea and talk about going up to Malakoff Diggings in Nevada County because some people are starting a commune there and Max thinks it would be a groove to take acid in the diggings. He says maybe we could go next week, or the week after, or anyway sometime before his case comes up. Almost everybody I meet in San Francisco has to go to court at some point in the middle future. I never ask why.

I am still interested in how Max got rid of his middle-class Freudian hang-ups and I ask if he is now completely free.

"Nah," he says. "I got acid."

Max drops a 250- or 350-microgram tab every six or seven days.

Max and Don share a joint in the car and we go over to North Beach to find out if Otto, who has a temporary job there, wants to go to Malakoff Diggings. Otto is pitching some electronics engineers. The engineers view our arrival with some interest, maybe, I think, because Max is wearing bells and an Indian headband. Max has a low tolerance for straight engineers and their Freudian hang-ups. "Look at 'em," he says. "They're always yelling 'queer' and then they come sneaking down to the Haight-Ashbury trying to get the hippie chick because she fucks."

We do not get around to asking Otto about Malakoff Diggings because he wants to tell me about a fourteen-year-old he knows who got busted in the Park the other day. She was just walking through the Park, he says, minding her own, carrying her schoolbooks, when the cops took her in and booked her and gave her a pelvic. *"Fourteen years old,"* Otto says. *"A pelvic."*

"Coming down from acid," he adds, "that could be a real bad trip."

I call Otto the next afternoon to see if he can reach the fourteen-year-old. It turns out she is tied up with rehearsals for her junior-high-school play, *The Wizard of Oz.* "Yellow-brick-road time," Otto says. Otto was sick all day. He thinks it was some cocaine-and-wheat somebody gave him.

There are always little girls around rock groups—the same little girls who used to hang around saxophone players, girls who live on the celebrity and power and sex a band projects when it plays—and there are three of them out here this afternoon in Sausalito where the Grateful Dead rehearse. They are all pretty and two of them still have baby fat and one of them dances by herself with her eyes closed.

I ask a couple of the girls what they do.

"I just kind of come out here a lot," one of them says.

"I just sort of know the Dead," the other says.

The one who just sort of knows the Dead starts cutting up a loaf of French bread on the piano bench. The boys take a break and one of them talks about playing the Los Angeles Cheetah, which is in the old Aragon Ballroom. "We were up there drinking beer where Lawrence Welk used to sit," Jerry Garcia says.

The little girl who was dancing by herself giggles. "Too much," she says softly. Her eyes are still closed.

Somebody said that if I was going to meet some runaways I better pick up a few hamburgers and Cokes on the way, so I did, and we are eating them in the Park together, me, Debbie who is fifteen, and Jeff who is sixteen. Debbie and Jeff ran away twelve days ago, walked out of school one morning with $100 between them. Because a missing-juvenile is out on Debbie—she was already on probation because her mother had once taken her down to the police station and declared her incorrigible—this is only the second time they have been out of a friend's apartment since they got to San Francisco. The first time they went over to the Fairmont Hotel and rode the outside elevator, three times up and three times down. "Wow," Jeff says, and that is all he can think to say, about that.

I ask why they ran away.

"My parents said I had to go to church," Debbie says. "And they wouldn't let me dress the way I wanted. In the seventh grade my skirts were longer than anybody's—it got better in the eighth grade, but still."

"Your mother was kind of a bummer," Jeff agrees.

"They didn't like Jeff. They didn't like my

girlfriends. My father thought I was cheap and he told me so. I had a C average and he told me I couldn't date until I raised it, and that bugged me too."

"My mother was just a genuine all-American bitch," Jeff says. "She was really troublesome about hair. Also she didn't like boots. It was really weird."

"Tell about the chores," Debbie says.

"For example I had chores. If I didn't finish ironing my shirts for the week I couldn't go out for the weekend. It was weird. Wow."

Debbie giggles and shakes her head. "This year's gonna be wild."

"We're just gonna let it all happen," Jeff says. "Everything's in the future, you can't pre-plan it. First we get jobs, then a place to live. Then, I dunno."

Jeff finishes off the French fries and gives some thought to what kind of job he could get. "I always kinda dug metal shop, welding, stuff like that." Maybe he could work on cars, I say. "I'm not too mechanically minded," he says. "Anyway you can't pre-plan."

"I could get a job baby-sitting," Debbie says. "Or in a dime store."

"You're always talking about getting a job in a dime store," Jeff says.

"That's because I worked in a dime store already."

Debbie is buffing her fingernails with the belt to her suède jacket. She is annoyed because she chipped a nail and because I do not have any polish remover in the car. I promise to get her to a friend's apartment so that she can redo her manicure, but something has been bothering me and as I fiddle with the ignition I finally ask it. I ask them to think back to when they were children, to tell me what they had wanted to be when they were grown up, how they had seen the future then.

Jeff throws a Coca-Cola bottle out the car window. "I can't remember I ever thought about it," he says.

"I remember I wanted to be a veterinarian once," Debbie says. "But now I'm more or less working in the vein of being an artist or a model or a cosmetologist. Or something."

I hear quite a bit about one cop, Officer Arthur Gerrans, whose name has become a synonym for zealotry on the Street. "He's our Officer Krupke," Max once told me. Max is not personally wild about Officer Gerrans because Officer Gerrans took Max in after the Human Be-In last winter, that's the big Human Be-In in Golden Gate Park where 20,000 people got turned on free, or 10,000 did, or some number did, but then Officer Gerrans has busted almost everyone in the District at one time or another. Presumably to forestall a cult of personality, Officer Gerrans was transferred out of the District not long ago, and when I see him it is not at the Park Station but at the Central Station on Greenwich Avenue.

We are in an interrogation room, and I am interrogating Officer Gerrans. He is young and blond and wary and I go in slow. I wonder what he thinks "the major problems" in the Haight are.

Officer Gerrans thinks it over. "I would

say the major problems there," he says finally, "the major problems are narcotics and juveniles. Juveniles and narcotics, those are your major problems."

I write that down.

"Just one moment," Officer Gerrans says, and leaves the room. When he comes back he tells me that I cannot talk to him without permission from Chief Thomas Cahill.

"In the meantime," Officer Gerrans adds, pointing at the notebook in which I have written *major problems: juveniles, narcotics,* "I'll take those notes."

The next day I apply for permission to talk to Officer Gerrans and also to Chief Cahill. A few days later a sergeant returns my call.

"We have finally received clearance from the Chief per your request," the sergeant says, "and that is taboo."

I wonder why it is taboo to talk to Officer Gerrans.

Officer Gerrans is involved in court cases coming to trial.

I wonder why it is taboo to talk to Chief Cahill.

The Chief has pressing police business.

I wonder if I can talk to anyone at all in the Police Department.

"No," the sergeant says, "not at the particular moment."

Which was my last official contact with the San Francisco Police Department.

Norris and I are standing around the Panhandle and Norris is telling me how it is all set up for a friend to take me to Big Sur. I say what I really want to do is spend a few days with Norris and his wife and the rest of the people in their house. Norris says it would be a lot easier if I'd take some acid. I say I'm unstable. Norris says all right, anyway, *grass*, and he squeezes my hand.

One day Norris asks how old I am. I tell him I am thirty-two. It takes a few minutes, but Norris rises to it. "Don't worry," he says at last. "There's old hippies too."

It is a pretty nice evening and nothing much happening and Max brings his old lady, Sharon, over to the Warehouse. The Warehouse, which is where Don and a floating number of other people live, is not actually a warehouse but the garage of a condemned hotel. The Warehouse was conceived as total theater, a continual happening, and I always feel good there. What happened ten minutes ago or what is going to happen a half hour from now tends to fade from mind in the Warehouse. Somebody is usually doing something interesting, like working on a light show, and there are a lot of interesting things around, like an old Chevrolet touring car which is used as a bed and a vast American flag fluttering up in the shadows and an overstuffed chair suspended like a swing from the rafters, the point of that being that it gives you a sensory-deprivation high.

One reason I particularly like the Warehouse is that a child named Michael is staying there now. Michael's mother, Sue

Ann, is a sweet wan girl who is always in the kitchen cooking seaweed or baking macrobiotic bread while Michael amuses himself with joss sticks or an old tambourine or a rocking horse with the paint worn off. The first time I ever saw Michael was on that rocking horse, a very blond and pale and dirty child on a rocking horse with no paint. A blue theatrical spotlight was the only light in the Warehouse that afternoon, and there was Michael in it, crooning softly to the wooden horse. Michael is three years old. He is a bright child but does not yet talk.

This particular night Michael is trying to light his joss sticks and there are the usual number of people floating through and they all drift into Don's room and sit on the bed and pass joints. Sharon is very excited when she arrives. "*Don,*" she cries, breathless. "We got some STP today." At this time STP is a pretty big deal, remember; nobody yet knew what it was and it was relatively, although just relatively, hard to come by. Sharon is blond and scrubbed and probably seventeen, but Max is a little vague about that since his court case comes up in a month or so and he doesn't need statutory rape on top of it. Sharon's parents were living apart when last she saw them. She does not miss school or anything much about her past, except her younger brother. "I want to turn him on," she confided one day. "He's fourteen now, that's the perfect age. I know where he goes to high school and someday I'll just go get him."

Time passes and I lose the thread and when I pick it up again Max seems to be talking about what a beautiful thing it is the way Sharon washes dishes.

"Well it *is* beautiful," Sharon says. "*Everything* is. I mean you watch that blue detergent blob run on the plate, watch the grease cut—well, it can be a real trip."

Pretty soon now, maybe next month, maybe later, Max and Sharon plan to leave for Africa and India, where they can live off the land. "I got this little trust fund, see," Max says, "which is useful in that it tells cops and border patrols I'm O.K., but living off the land is the thing. You can get your high and get your dope in the city, O.K., but we gotta get out somewhere and live organically."

"Roots and things," Sharon says, lighting another joss stick for Michael. Michael's mother is still in the kitchen cooking seaweed. "You can eat them."

Maybe eleven o'clock, we move from the Warehouse to the place where Max and Sharon live with a couple named Tom and Barbara. Sharon is pleased to get home ("I hope you got some hash joints fixed in the kitchen," she says to Barbara by way of greeting) and everybody is pleased to show off the apartment, which has a lot of flowers and candles and paisleys. Max and Sharon and Tom and Barbara get pretty high on hash, and everyone dances a little and we do some liquid projections and set up a strobe and take turns getting a high on that. Quite late, somebody called Steve comes in with a pretty, dark girl. They have been to a meeting of people who practice a Western yoga, but they do not seem to want to talk about that. They lie on the floor awhile, and then Steve stands up.

"Max," he says, "I want to say one thing."

"It's your trip." Max is edgy.

"I found love on acid. But I lost it. And now I'm finding it again. With nothing but grass."

Max mutters that heaven and hell are both in one's karma.

"That's what bugs me about psychedelic art," Steve says.

"What about psychedelic art," Max says. "I haven't seen much psychedelic art."

Max is lying on a bed with Sharon, and Steve leans down to him. "Groove, baby," he says. "You're a groove."

Steve sits down then and tells me about one summer when he was at a school of design in Rhode Island and took thirty trips, the last ones all bad. I ask why they were bad. "I could tell you it was my neuroses," he says, "but fuck that."

A few days later I drop by to see Steve in his apartment. He paces nervously around the room he uses as a studio and shows me some paintings. We do not seem to be getting to the point.

"Maybe you noticed something going on at Max's," he says abruptly.

It seems that the girl he brought, the dark pretty one, had once been Max's girl. She had followed him to Tangier and now to San Francisco. But Max has Sharon. "So she's kind of staying around here," Steve says.

Steve is troubled by a lot of things. He is twenty-three, was raised in Virginia, and has the idea that California is the beginning of the end. "I feel it's insane," he says, and his voice drops. "This chick tells me there's no meaning to life but it doesn't matter, we'll just flow right out. There've been times I felt like packing up and taking off for the East Coast again, at least there I had a *target*. At least there you expect that it's going to *happen*." He lights a cigarette for me and his hands shake. "Here you know it's not going to."

I ask what it is that is supposed to happen.

"I don't know," he says. "Something. Anything."

Arthur Lisch is on the telephone in his kitchen, trying to sell VISTA a program for the District. "We already *got* an emergency," he says into the telephone, meanwhile trying to disentangle his daughter, age one and a half, from the cord. "We don't get help here, nobody can guarantee what's going to happen. We've got people sleeping in the streets here. We've got people starving to death." He pauses. "All right," he says then, and his voice rises. "So they're doing it by choice. So what."

By the time he hangs up he has limned what strikes me as a pretty Dickensian picture of life on the edge of Golden Gate Park, but then this is my first exposure to Arthur Lisch's "riot-on-the-Street-unless" pitch. Arthur Lisch is a kind of leader of the Diggers, who, in the official District mythology, are supposed to be a group of anonymous good guys with no thought in their collective head but to lend a helping hand. The official District mythology also has it that the Diggers have no "leaders," but nonetheless Arthur Lisch is one. Arthur Lisch is also a paid worker for the American Friends' Service Committee and he lives with his wife, Jane, and their two small children in a railroad flat, which on this particular day lacks organization. For one thing the telephone keeps ringing. Arthur promises to attend a hearing at city hall. Arthur promises to "send Edward, he's O.K." Arthur promises to get a good group, maybe the Loading Zone, to play free for a Jewish benefit. For a second thing the baby is crying, and she does not stop until Jane Lisch appears with a jar of Gerber's Junior Chicken Noodle Dinner. Another confusing element is somebody named Bob, who just sits in the living room and looks at his toes. First he looks at the toes on one foot, then at the toes on the other. I make several attempts to include Bob in the conversation before I realize he is on a bad trip. Moreover, there are two people hacking up what looks like a side of beef on the kitchen floor, the idea being that when it gets hacked up, Jane Lisch can cook it for the daily Digger feed in the Park.

Arthur Lisch does not seem to notice any of this. He just keeps talking about cybernated societies and the guaranteed annual wage and riot on the Street, unless.

I call the Lisches a day or so later and ask for Arthur. Jane Lisch says he's next door taking a shower because somebody is coming down from a bad trip in their bathroom. Besides the freak-out in the bathroom they are expecting a psychiatrist in to look at Bob. Also a doctor for Edward, who is not O.K. at all but has the flu. Jane says maybe I should talk to Chester Anderson. She will not give me his number.

Chester Anderson is a legacy of the Beat Generation, a man in his middle thirties whose peculiar hold on the District derives from his possession of a mimeograph machine, on which he prints communiqués signed "the communication company." It is another tenet of the official District mythology that the communication company will print anything anybody has to say, but in fact Chester Anderson prints only what he writes himself, agrees with, or considers harmless or dead matter. His statements, which are left in piles and pasted on windows around Haight Street, are regarded with some apprehension in the District and with considerable interest by outsiders, who study them, like China watchers, for subtle shifts in obscure ideologies. An Anderson communiqué might be doing something as specific as fingering someone who is said to have set up a marijuana bust, or it might be working in a more general vein:

> Pretty little 16-year-old middle-class chick comes to the Haight to see what it's all about & gets picked up by a 17-year-old street dealer who spends all day shooting her full of speed again & again, then feeds her 3,000 mikes & raffles off her temporarily unemployed body for the biggest Haight Street gangbang since the night before last. The politics and ethics of ecstasy. Rape is as common as bullshit on Haight Street. Kids are starving on the Street. Minds and

bodies are being maimed as we watch, a scale model of Vietnam.

Somebody other than Jane Lisch gave me an address for Chester Anderson, 443 Arguello, but 443 Arguello does not exist. I telephone the wife of the man who gave me 443 Arguello and she says it's 742 Arguello.

"But don't go up there," she says.

I say I'll telephone.

"There's no number," she says. "I can't give it to you."

"742 Arguello," I say.

"No," she says. "I don't know. And don't go there. And don't use either my name or my husband's name if you do."

She is the wife of a full professor of English at San Francisco State College. I decide to lie low on the question of Chester Anderson for awhile.

Paranoia strikes deep—
Into your life it will creep—
        is a song the Buffalo
        Springfield sings.

The appeal of Malakoff Diggings has kind of faded out but Max says why don't I come to his place, just be there, the next time he takes acid. Tom will take it too, probably Sharon, maybe Barbara. We can't do it for six or seven days because Max and Tom are in STP space now. They are not crazy about STP but it has advantages. "You've still got your forebrain," Tom says. "I could write behind STP, but not behind acid." This is the first time I have heard of anything you can't do behind acid, also the first time I have heard that Tom writes.

Otto is feeling better because he discovered it wasn't the cocaine-and-wheat that made him sick. It was the chicken pox, which he caught baby-sitting for Big Brother and the Holding Company one night when they were playing. I go over to see him and meet Vicki, who sings now and then with a group called the Jook Savages and lives at Otto's place. Vicki dropped out of Laguna High "because I had mono," followed the Grateful Dead up to San Francisco one time and has been here "for a while." Her mother and father are divorced, and she does not see her father, who works for a network in New York. A few months ago he came out to do a documentary on the District and tried to find her, but couldn't. Later he wrote her a letter in care of her mother urging her to go back to school. Vicki guesses maybe she will sometime but she doesn't see much point in it right now.

We are eating a little tempura in Japantown, Chet Helms and I, and he is sharing some of his insights with me. Until a couple of years ago Chet Helms never did much besides hitchhiking, but now he runs the Avalon Ballroom and flies over the Pole to check out the London scene and says things like "Just for the sake of clarity I'd like to categorize the aspects of primitive religion as I see it." Right now he is talking about

Marshall McLuhan and how the printed word is finished, out, over. "The *East Village Other* is one of the few papers in America whose books are in the black," he says. "I know that from reading *Barron's*."

A new group is supposed to play in the Panhandle today but they are having trouble with the amplifier and I sit in the sun listening to a couple of little girls, maybe seventeen years old. One of them has a lot of makeup and the other wears Levi's and cowboy boots. The boots do not look like an affectation, they look like she came up off a ranch about two weeks ago. I wonder what she is doing here in the Panhandle trying to make friends with a city girl who is snubbing her but I do not wonder long, because she is homely and awkward and I think of her going all the way through the consolidated union high school out there where she comes from and nobody ever asking her to go into Reno on Saturday night for a drive-in movie and a beer on the riverbank, so she runs. "I know a thing about dollar bills," she is saying now. "You get one that says '1111' in one corner and '1111' in another, you take it down to Dallas, Texas, they'll give you $15 for it."

"Who will?" the city girl asks.

"I don't know."

"There are only three significant pieces of data in the world today," is another thing Chet Helms told me one night. We were at the Avalon and the big strobe was going and the colored lights and the Day-Glo painting and the place was full of high-school kids trying to look turned on. The Avalon sound system projects 126 decibels at 100 feet but to Chet Helms the sound is just there, like the air, and he talks through it. "The first is," he said, "God died last year and was obited by the press. The second is, fifty percent of the population is or will be under twenty-five." A boy shook a tambourine toward us and Chet smiled benevolently at him. "The third," he said, "is that they got twenty billion irresponsible dollars to spend."

Thursday comes, some Thursday, and Max and Tom and Sharon and maybe Barbara are going to take some acid. They want to drop it about three o'clock. Barbara has baked fresh bread, Max has gone to the Park for fresh flowers, and Sharon is making a sign for the door which reads "DO NOT DISTURB, RING, KNOCK, OR IN ANY OTHER WAY DISTURB. LOVE." This is not how I would put it to either the health inspector, who is due this week, or any of the several score narcotics agents in the neighborhood, but I figure the sign is Sharon's trip.

Once the sign is finished Sharon gets restless. "Can I at least play the new record?" she asks Max.

"Tom and Barbara want to save it for when we're high."

"I'm getting bored, just sitting around here."

Max watches her jump up and walk out.

"That's what you call pre-acid uptight jitters," he says.

Barbara is not in evidence. Tom keeps walking in and out. "All these innumerable last-minute things you have to do," he mutters.

"It's a tricky thing, acid," Max says after a while. He is turning the stereo on and off. "When a chick takes acid, it's all right if she's alone, but when she's living with somebody this edginess comes out. And if the hour-and-a-half process before you take the acid doesn't go smooth . . ." He picks up a roach and studies it, then adds, "They're having a little thing back there with Barbara."

Sharon and Tom walk in.

"You pissed off too?" Max asks Sharon.

Sharon does not answer.

Max turns to Tom. "Is she all right?"

"Yeh."

"Can we take acid?" Max is on edge.

"I don't know what she's going to do."

"What do you want to do?"

"What I want to do depends on what she wants to do." Tom is rolling some joints, first rubbing the papers with a marijuana resin he makes himself. He takes the joints back to the bedroom, and Sharon goes with him.

"Something like this happens every time people take acid," Max says. After a while he brightens and develops a theory around it. "Some people don't like to go out of themselves, that's the trouble. You probably wouldn't. You'd probably like only a quarter of a tab. There's still an ego on a quarter tab, and it wants things. Now if that thing is balling—and your old lady or your old man is off somewhere flashing and doesn't want to be touched—well, you get put down on acid, you can be on a bummer for months."

Sharon drifts in, smiling. "Barbara might take some acid, we're all feeling better, we smoked a joint."

At three-thirty that afternoon Max, Tom, and Sharon placed tabs under their tongues and sat down together in the living room to wait for the flash. Barbara stayed in the bedroom, smoking hash. During the next four hours a window banged once in Barbara's room, and about five-thirty some children had a fight on the street. A curtain billowed in the afternoon wind. A cat scratched a beagle in Sharon's lap. Except for the sitar music on the stereo there was no other sound or movement until seven-thirty, when Max said "Wow."

I spot Deadeye on Haight Street, and he gets in the car. Until we get off the Street he sits very low and inconspicuous. Deadeye wants me to meet his old lady, but first he wants to talk to me about how he got hip to helping people.

"Here I was, just a tough kid on a motor-cycle," he says, "and suddenly I see that young people don't have to walk alone." Deadeye has a clear evangelistic gaze and the reasonable rhetoric of a car salesman. He is society's model product. I try to meet his gaze directly because he once told me he could read character in people's eyes, particularly if he has just dropped acid, which he did, about nine o'clock this morning. "They just have to remember one thing," he says. "The Lord's Prayer. And that can help them in more ways than one."

He takes a much-folded letter from his wallet. The letter is from a little girl he helped. "My loving brother," it begins. "I thought I'd write you a letter since I'm a part of you. Remember that: When you feel happiness, I do, when you feel . . ."

"What I want to do now," Deadeye says, "is set up a house where a person of any age can come, spend a few days, talk over his problems. *Any age*. People your age, they've got problems too."

I say a house will take money.

"I've found a way to make money," Deadeye says. He hesitates only a few seconds. "I could've made eighty-five dollars on the Street just then. See, in my pocket I had a hundred tabs of acid. I had to come up with twenty dollars by tonight or we're out of the house we're in, so I knew somebody who had acid, and I knew somebody who wanted it, so I made the connection."

Since the Mafia moved into the LSD racket, the quantity is up and the quality is down... Historian Arnold Toynbee celebrated his 78th birthday Friday night by snapping his fingers and tapping his toes to the Quicksilver Messenger Service... are a couple of items from Herb Caen's column one morning as the West declined in the spring of 1967.

When I was in San Francisco a tab, or a cap, of LSD-25 sold for three to five dollars, depending upon the seller and the district. LSD was slightly cheaper in the Haight-Ashbury than in the Fillmore, where it was used rarely, mainly as a sexual ploy, and sold by pushers of hard drugs, e.g., heroin, or "smack." A great deal of acid was being cut with Methedrine, which is the trade name for an amphetamine, because Methedrine can simulate the flash that low-quality acid lacks. Nobody knows how much LSD is actually in a tab, but the standard trip is supposed to be 250 micrograms. Grass was running ten dollars a lid, five dollars a matchbox. Hash was considered "a luxury item." All the amphetamines, or "speed"—Benzedrine, Dexedrine, and particularly Methedrine—were in far more common use in the late spring than they had been in the early spring. Some attributed this to the presence of the Syndicate; others to a general deterioration of the scene, to the incursions of gangs and younger part-time, or "plastic," hippies, who like the amphetamines and the illusions of action and power they give. Where Methedrine is in wide use, heroin tends to be available, because, I was told, "You can get awful damn high shooting crystal, and smack can be used to bring you down."

Deadeye's old lady, Gerry, meets us at the door of their place. She is a big, hearty girl who has always counseled at Girl Scout camps during summer vacations and was "in social welfare" at the University of Washington when she decided that she "just hadn't done enough living" and came to San Francisco. "Actually the heat was bad in Seattle," she adds.

"The first night I got down here," she says, "I stayed with a gal I met over at the Blue Unicorn. I looked like I'd just arrived, had a knapsack and stuff." After that, Gerry stayed at a house the Diggers were running, where she met Deadeye. "Then it took time to get my bearings, so I haven't done much work yet."

I ask Gerry what work she does. "Basically I'm a poet," she says, "but I had my guitar stolen right after I arrived, and that kind of hung up my thing."

"Get your books," Deadeye orders. "Show her your books."

Gerry demurs, then goes into the bedroom and comes back with several theme books full of verse. I leaf through them but Deadeye is still talking about helping people. "Any kid that's on speed," he says, "I'll try to get him off it. The only advantage to it from the kids' point of view is that you don't have to worry about sleeping or eating."

"Or sex," Gerry adds.

"That's right. When you're strung out on crystal you don't need *nothing*."

"It can lead to the hard stuff," Gerry says. "Take your average Meth freak, once he's started putting the needle in his arm, it's not too hard to say, well, let's shoot a little smack."

All the while I am looking at Gerry's poems. They are a very young girl's poems, each written out in a neat hand and finished off with a curlicue. Dawns are roseate, skies silver-tinted. When Gerry writes "crystal" in her books, she does not mean Meth.

"You gotta get back to your writing," Deadeye says fondly, but Gerry ignores this. She is telling about somebody who propositioned her yesterday. "He just walked up to me on the Street, offered me six hundred dollars to go to Reno and do the thing."

"You're not the only one he approached," Deadeye says.

"If some chick wants to go with him, fine,"

Gerry says. "Just don't bum my trip." She empties the tuna-fish can we are using for an ashtray and goes over to look at a girl who is asleep on the floor. It is the same girl who was sleeping on the floor the first day I came to Deadeye's place. She has been sick a week now, ten days. "Usually when somebody comes up to me on the Street like that," Gerry adds, "I hit him for some change."

When I saw Gerry in the Park the next day I asked her about the sick girl, and Gerry said cheerfully that she was in the hospital, with pneumonia.

Max tells me about how he and Sharon got together. "When I saw her the first time on Haight Street, I flashed. I mean flashed. So I started some conversation with her about her beads, see, but I didn't care about her beads." Sharon lived in a house where a friend of Max's lived, and the next time he saw her was when he took the friend some bananas. "It was during the great banana bubble. You had to kind of force your personality and the banana peels down their throats. Sharon and I were like kids—we just smoked bananas and looked at each other and smoked more bananas and looked at each other."

But Max hesitated. For one thing he thought Sharon was his friend's girl. "For another I didn't know if I wanted to get hung up with an old lady." But the next time he visited the house, Sharon was on acid.

"So everybody yelled 'Here comes the banana man,'" Sharon interrupts, "and I got all excited."

"She was living in this crazy house," Max continues. "There was this one kid, all he did was scream. His whole trip was to practice screams. It was too much." Max still hung back from Sharon. "But then she offered me a tab, and I knew."

Max walked to the kitchen and back with the tab, wondering whether to take it. "And then I decided to flow with it, and that was that. Because once you drop acid with somebody you flash on, you see the whole world melt in her eyes."

"It's stronger than anything in the world," Sharon says.

"Nothing can break it up," Max says. "As long as it lasts."

> *No milk today—*
> *My love has gone away . . .*
> *The end of my hopes—*
> *The end of all my dreams—*
> is a song I heard every morning in the
> cold late spring of 1967 on KFRC, the
> Flower Power Station, San Francisco.

Deadeye and Gerry tell me they plan to be married. An Episcopal priest in the District has promised to perform the wedding in Golden Gate Park, and they will have a few rock groups there, "a real community thing." Gerry's brother is also getting married, in Seattle. "Kind of interesting," Gerry

muses, "because, you know, his is the traditional straight wedding, and then you have
the contrast with ours."

"I'll have to wear a tie to his," Deadeye
says.

"Right," Gerry says.

"Her parents came down to meet me, but
they weren't ready for me," Deadeye notes
philosophically.

"They finally gave it their blessing,"
Gerry says. "In a way."

"They came to me and her father said,
'Take care of her,'" Deadeye reminisces.
"And her mother said, 'Don't let her go to
jail.'"

Barbara baked a macrobiotic apple pie and
she and Tom and Max and Sharon and I are
eating it. Barbara tells me how she learned
to find happiness in "the woman's thing."
She and Tom had gone somewhere to live
with the Indians, and although she first
found it hard to be shunted off with the
women and never to enter into any of the

men's talk, she soon got the point. "That was where the *trip* was," she says.

"Barbara is on what is called the woman's trip to the exclusion of almost everything else. When she and Tom and Max and Sharon need money, Barbara will take a part-time job, modeling or teaching kindergarten, but she dislikes earning more than ten or twenty dollars a week. Most of the time she keeps house and bakes. "Doing something that shows your love that way," she says, "is just about the most beautiful thing I know." Whenever I hear about the woman's trip, which is often, I think a lot about nothin'-says-lovin'-like-something-from-the-oven and the Feminine Mystique and how it is possible for people to be the unconscious instruments of values they would strenuously reject on a conscious level, but I do not mention this to Barbara.

It is a pretty nice day and I am just driving down the Street and I see Barbara at a light.

What am I doing, she wants to know.

I am just driving around.

"Groovy," she says.

It's a beautiful day, I say.

"Groovy," she agrees.

She wants to know if I will come over.
Sometime soon, I say.

"Groovy," she says.

I ask if she wants to drive in the Park but
she is too busy. She is out to buy wool for
her loom.

Arthur Lisch gets pretty nervous whenever
he sees me now because the Digger line this
week is that they aren't talking to "media
poisoners," which is me. So I still don't have
a tap on Chester Anderson, but one day
in the Panhandle I run into a kid he says
he is Chester's "associate." He has on a
black cape, black slouch hat, mauve Job's
Daughters sweatshirt and dark glasses, and
he says his name is Claude Hayward, but
never mind that because I think of him just

as The Connection. The Connection offers to "check me out."

I take off my dark glasses so he can see my eyes. He leaves his on.

"How much you get paid for doing this kind of media poisoning?" he says for openers.

I put my dark glasses back on.

"There's only one way to find out where it's at," The Connection says, and jerks his thumb at the photographer I'm with. "Dump him and get out on the Street. Don't take money. You won't need money." He reaches into his cape and pulls out a Mimeographed sheet announcing a series of classes at the Digger Free Store on How to Avoid Getting Busted, Gangbangs, VD, Rape, Pregnancy, Beatings, and Starvation. "You oughta come," The Connection says. "You'll need it."

I say maybe, but meanwhile I would like to talk to Chester Anderson.

"If we decide to get in touch with you at all," The Connection says, "we'll get in touch with you real quick." He kept an eye on me in the Park after that but never called the number I gave him.

It is twilight and cold and too early to find Deadeye at the Blue Unicorn so I ring Max's bell. Barbara comes to the door.

"Max and Tom are seeing somebody on a kind of business thing," she says. "Can you come back a little later?"

I am hard put to think what Max and Tom might be seeing somebody about in the way of business, but a few days later in the Park I find out.

"Hey," Max calls. "Sorry you couldn't come up the other day, but *business* was being done." This time I get the point. "We got some great stuff," he says, and begins to elaborate. Every third person in the Park this afternoon looks like a narcotics agent and I try to change the subject. Later I suggest to Max that he be more wary in public. "Listen, I'm very cautious," he says. "You can't be too careful."

By now I have an unofficial taboo contact
with the San Francisco Police Department.
What happens is that this cop and I meet
in various late-movie ways, like I happen to
be sitting in the bleachers at a baseball game
and he happens to sit down next to me, and
we exchange guarded generalities. No information actually passes between us, but
after a while we get to kind of like each
other.

"The kids aren't too bright," he is telling
me on this particular day. "They'll tell you
they can always spot an undercover, they'll
tell you about 'the kind of car he drives.' They
aren't talking about undercovers, they're
talking about plainclothesmen who just happen to drive unmarked cars, like I do. They
can't tell an undercover. An undercover
doesn't drive some black Ford with a two-
way radio."

He tells me about an undercover who
was taken out of the District because he was
believed to be overexposed, too familiar.

He was transferred to the narcotics squad, and by error was sent immediately back into the District as a narcotics undercover.

The cop plays with his keys. "You want to know how smart these kids are?" he says finally. "The first week, this guy makes forty-three cases."

The Jook Savages are supposed to be having a May Day party in Larkspur and I go by the Warehouse and Don and Sue Ann think it would be nice to drive over there because Sue Ann's three-year-old, Michael, hasn't been out lately. The air is soft and there is a sunset haze around the Golden Gate and Don asks Sue Ann how many flavors she can detect in a single grain of rice and Sue Ann tells Don maybe she better learn to cook *yang*, maybe they are all too *yin* at the Warehouse, and I try to teach Michael "Frère Jacques." We each have our own trip and it is a nice drive. Which is just as well because there is nobody at all at the Jook Savages' place, not even the Jook Savages. When we get back Sue Ann decides to cook up a lot of apples they have around the Warehouse and Don starts working with his light show and I go down to see Max for a minute. "Out of sight," Max says about the Larkspur caper. "Somebody thinks it would be groovy to turn on five hundred people the first day in May, and it would be, but then they turn on the last day in April instead, so it doesn't happen. If it happens, it happens. If it doesn't, it doesn't. Who cares. Nobody cares."

Some kid with braces on his teeth is playing his guitar and boasting that he got the last of the STP from Mr. O. himself and somebody else is talking about how five grams of acid will be liberated within the next month and you can see that nothing much is happening this afternoon around the *San Francisco Oracle* office. A boy sits at a drawing board drawing the infinitesimal figures that people do on speed, and the kid with the braces watches him. *"I'm gonna*

shoot my wo—man," he sings softly. *"She been with a—noth—er man."* Someone works out the numerology of my name and the name of the photographer I'm with. The photographer's is all white and the sea ("If I were to make you some beads, see, I'd do it mainly in white," he is told), but mine has a double death symbol. The afternoon does not seem to be getting anywhere, so it is suggested that we go over to Japantown and find somebody named Sandy who will take us to the Zen temple.

Four boys and one middle-aged man are sitting on a grass mat at Sandy's place, sipping anise tea and watching Sandy read Laura Huxley's *You Are Not the Target.*

We sit down and have some anise tea. "Meditation turns us on," Sandy says. He has a shaved head and the kind of cherubic face usually seen in newspaper photographs of mass murderers. The middle-aged man, whose name is George, is making me uneasy because he is in a trance next to me and stares at me without seeing me.

I feel that my mind is going—George is *dead*, or we *all* are—when the telephone rings.

"It's for George," Sandy says.

"George, *tele*phone."

"*George*."

Somebody waves his hand in front of George and George finally gets up, bows, and moves toward the door on the balls of his feet.

"I think I'll take George's tea," somebody says. "George—are you coming back?"

George stops at the door and stares at each of us in turn. "In a *moment*," he snaps.

Do you know who is the first eternal
  spaceman of this universe?
The first to send his wild wild vibrations
To all those cosmic superstations?
For the song he always shouts
Sends the planets flipping out . . .
But I'll tell you before you think me loony
That I'm talking about Narada Muni . . .

Singing

HARE KRISHNA   HARE KRISHNA
KRISHNA KRISHNA HARE HARE
HARE RAMA   HARE RAMA
RAMA RAMA HARE HARE

is a Krishna song. Words by
Howard Wheeler and music by
Michael Grant.

Maybe the trip is not in Zen but in
Krishna, so I pay a visit to Michael Grant, the
Swami A.C. Bhaktivedanta's leading disciple
in San Francisco. Michael Grant is at home
with his brother-in-law and his wife, a pretty
girl wearing a cashmere pullover, a jumper,
and a red caste mark on her forehead.

"I've been associated with the Swami
since about last July," Michael says. "See, the
Swami came here from India and he was at
this ashram in upstate New York and he
just kept to himself and chanted a lot. For a
couple of months. Pretty soon I helped him
get his storefront in New York. Now it's an
international movement, which we spread
by teaching this chant." Michael is fingering
his red wooden beads and I notice that I am

the only person in the room with shoes on. "It's catching on like wildfire."

"If everybody chanted," the brother-in-law says, "there wouldn't be any problem with the police or anybody."

"Ginsberg calls the chant ecstasy, but the Swami says that's not exactly it." Michael walks across the room and straightens a picture of Krishna as a baby. "Too bad you can't meet the Swami," he adds. "The Swami's in New York now."

"Ecstasy's not the right word at all," says the brother-in-law, who has been thinking about it. "It makes you think of some . . . mun*dane* ecstasy."

The next day I drop by Max and Sharon's, and find them in bed smoking a little morning hash. Sharon once advised me that half a joint even of grass would make getting up in the morning a beautiful thing. I ask Max how Krishna strikes him.

"You can get a high on a mantra," he says. "But I'm holy on acid."

Max passes the joint to Sharon and leans back. "Too bad you couldn't meet the Swami," he says. "The Swami was the turn-on."

Anybody who thinks this is all about drugs has his head in a bag. It's a social movement, quintessentially romantic, the kind that recurs in times of real social crisis. The themes are always the same. A return to innocence. The invocation of an earlier authority and control. The mysteries of the blood. An itch for the transcendental, for purification. Right there you've got the ways that romanticism historically ends up in trouble, lends itself to authoritarianism. When the direction appears. How long do you think it'll take for that to happen? is a question a San Francisco psychiatrist asked me.

At the time I was in San Francisco the political potential of what was then called the movement was just becoming clear. It had always been clear to the revolutionary core of the Diggers, whose every guerrilla talent was now bent toward open confrontations and the creation of a summer emergency, and it was clear to many of the straight doctors and priests and sociologists who had occasion to work in the District, and it could rapidly become clear to any outsider who bothered to decode Chester Anderson's call-to-action communiqués or to watch who was there first at the street skirmishes which now set the tone for life in the District. One did not have to be a political analyst to see it; the boys in the rock groups saw it, because they were often where it was happening. "In the Park there are always twenty or thirty people below the stand," one of the Dead complained to me. "Ready to take the crowd on some militant trip."

But the peculiar beauty of this political potential, as far as the activists were concerned, was that it remained not clear at all to most of the inhabitants of the District, perhaps because the few seventeen-year-olds who are political realists tend not to adopt romantic idealism as a life style. Nor was it clear to the press, which at varying levels of competence continued to report "the hippie phenomenon" as an extended panty raid; an artistic avant-garde led by such comfortable YMHA regulars as Allen Ginsberg; or a thoughtful protest, not unlike joining the Peace Corps, against the culture which had produced Saran-Wrap and the Vietnam War. This last, or they're-trying-to-tell-us-something approach, reached its apogee in a *Time* cover story which revealed that hippies "scorn money—they call it 'bread'" and remains the most remarkable, if unwitting, extant evidence that the signals between the generations are irrevocably jammed.

Because the signals the press was getting were immaculate of political possibilities, the tensions of the District went unremarked upon, even during the period when there were so many observers on Haight Street from *Life* and *Look* and CBS that they were largely observing one another. The observers believed roughly what the children told them: that they were a generation dropped out of political action, beyond power games, that the New Left was just another ego trip. *Ergo*, there really were no activists in the Haight-Ashbury, and those things which happened every Sunday were spontaneous demonstrations because, just as the Diggers say, the police are brutal and juveniles have no rights and runaways are deprived of their right to self-determination and people are starving to death on Haight Street, a scale model of Vietnam.

Of course the activists—not those whose thinking had become rigid, but those whose approach to revolution was imaginatively anarchic—had long ago grasped the reality which still eluded the press: we were seeing something important. We were seeing the desperate attempt of a handful of pathetically unequipped children to create a community in a social vacuum. Once we had seen these children, we could no longer overlook the vacuum, no longer pretend that the society's atomization could be reversed. This was not a traditional generational rebellion. At some point between 1945 and 1967 we had somehow neglected to tell these children the rules of the game we happened to be playing. Maybe we had stopped believing in the rules ourselves, maybe we were having a failure of nerve about the game. Maybe there were just too few people around to do the telling. These were children who grew up cut loose from the web of cousins and great-aunts and family doctors and lifelong neighbors who had traditionally suggested and enforced the society's values. They are children who have moved around a lot, *San Jose, Chula Vista, here.* They are less in rebellion against the society than ignorant of it, able only to feed back certain of its most publicized self-doubts, *Vietnam, Saran-Wrap, diet pills, the Bomb.*

They feed back exactly what is given them. Because they do not believe in words—words are for "typeheads," Chester Anderson tells them, and a thought which needs words is just one more of those ego trips—their only proficient vocabulary is in the society's platitudes. As it happens I am still committed to the idea that the ability to think for one's self depends upon one's mastery of the language, and I am not optimistic about children who will settle for saying, to indicate that their mother and father do not live together, that they come from "a broken home." They are sixteen, fifteen, fourteen years old, younger all the time, an army of children waiting to be given the words.

Peter Berg knows a lot of words.

"Is Peter Berg around?" I ask.

"Maybe."

"Are you Peter Berg?"

"Yeh."

The reason Peter Berg does not bother sharing too many words with me is because two of the words he knows are "media poisoning." Peter Berg wears a gold earring and is perhaps the only person in the District on whom a gold earring looks obscurely ominous. He belongs to the San Francisco Mime Troupe, some of whose members started the Artist's Liberation Front for "those who seek to combine their creative urge with socio-political involvement." It was out of the Mime Troupe that the Diggers grew, during the 1966 Hunter's Point riots, when it seemed a good idea to give away food and do puppet shows in the streets making fun of the National Guard. Along with Arthur Lisch, Peter Berg is part of the shadow leadership of the Diggers, and it was he who more or less invented and first introduced to the press the notion that there would be an influx into San Francisco during the summer of 1967 of 200,000 indigent adolescents. The only conversation I ever have with Peter Berg is about how he holds me personally responsible for the way *Life* captioned Henri Cartier-Bresson's pictures out of Cuba, but I like to watch him at work in the Park.

Janis Joplin is singing with Big Brother in the Panhandle and almost everybody is high and it is a pretty nice Sunday afternoon between three and six o'clock, which the activists say are the three hours of the week when something is most likely to happen in the Haight-Ashbury, and who turns up but Peter Berg. He is with his wife and six or seven other people, along with Chester Anderson's associate The Connection, and the first peculiar thing is, they're in blackface.

I mention to Max and Sharon that some members of the Mime Troupe seem to be in blackface.

"It's street theater," Sharon assures me. "It's supposed to be really groovy."

The Mime Troupers get a little closer, and there are some other peculiar things about them. For one thing they are tapping people on the head with dime-store plastic nightsticks, and for another they are wearing signs on their backs. "HOW MANY TIMES YOU BEEN RAPED, YOU LOVE FREAKS?" and "WHO STOLE CHUCK BERRY'S MUSIC?", things like that. Then they are distributing communication company fliers which say:

& this summer thousands of un-white un-suburban boppers are going to want to know why you've given up what they can't get & how you get away with it & how come you not a faggot with hair so long & they want haight street one way or the other. IF YOU DON'T KNOW, BY AUGUST HAIGHT STREET WILL BE A CEMETERY.

Max reads the flier and stands up. "I'm getting bad vibes," he says, and he and Sharon leave.

I have to stay around because I'm looking for Otto so I walk over to where the Mime Troupers have formed a circle around a Negro. Peter Berg is saying if anybody asks that this is street theater, and I figure the curtain is up because what they are doing right now is jabbing the Negro with the nightsticks. They jab, and they bare their teeth, and they rock on the balls of their feet and they wait.

"I'm beginning to get annoyed here," the Negro says. "I'm gonna get mad."

By now there are several Negroes around, reading the signs and watching.

"Just beginning to get annoyed, are you?" one of the Mime Troupers says. "Don't you think it's about time?"

"Nobody *stole* Chuck Berry's music, man," says another Negro who has been studying the signs. "Chuck Berry's music belongs to *everybody*."

"Yeh?" a girl in blackface says. "Everybody *who*?"

"Why," he says, confused. "Everybody. In America."

"In *America*," the blackface girl shrieks. "Listen to him talk about *America*."

"Listen," he says helplessly. "Listen here."

"What'd *America* ever do for you?" the girl in blackface jeers. "White kids here, they can sit in the Park all summer long, listening to the music they stole, because their bigshot parents keep sending them money. Who ever sends *you* money?"

"Listen," the Negro says, his voice rising. "You're gonna start something here, this isn't right—"

"You tell us what's right, black boy," the girl says.

The youngest member of the blackface group, an earnest tall kid about nineteen, twenty, is hanging back at the edge of the scene. I offer him an apple and ask what is going on. "Well," he says, "I'm new at this, I'm just beginning to study it, but you see the capitalists are taking over the District, and that's what Peter—well, ask Peter."

I did not ask Peter. It went on for a while. But on that particular Sunday between three and six o'clock everyone was too high and the weather was too good and the Hunter's Point gangs who usually come in between three and six on Sunday afternoon had come in on Saturday instead, and nothing started. While I waited for Otto I asked a little girl I knew slightly what she had thought of it. "It's something groovy they call street theater," she said. I said I had wondered if it might not have political overtones. She was seventeen years old and she worked it around in her mind awhile and finally she remembered a couple of words from somewhere. "Maybe it's some John Birch thing," she said.

When I finally find Otto he says "I got something at my place that'll blow your mind," and when we get there I see a child on the living-room floor, wearing a reefer

coat, reading a comic book. She keeps lick-
ing her lips in concentration and the only off
thing about her is that she's wearing white
lipstick.

"Five years old," Otto says. "On acid."

The five-year-old's name is Susan, and
she tells me she is in High Kindergarten.
She lives with her mother and some other
people, just got over the measles, wants a bi-
cycle for Christmas, and particularly likes
Coca-Cola, ice cream, Marty in the Jeffer-
son Airplane, Bob in the Grateful Dead,
and the beach. She remembers going to the
beach once a long time ago, and wishes she
had taken a bucket. For a year now her
mother has given her both acid and peyote.
Susan describes it as getting stoned.

I start to ask if any of the other children
in High Kindergarten get stoned, but I fal-
ter at the key words.

"She means do the other kids in your
class turn on, *get stoned*," says the friend of
her mother's who brought her to Otto's.

"Only Sally and Anne," Susan says.

"What about Lia?" her mother's friend
prompts.

"Lia," Susan says, "is not in High Kindergarten."

Sue Ann's three-year-old Michael started a fire this morning before anyone was up, but Don got it out before much damage was done. Michael burned his arm though, which is probably why Sue Ann was so jumpy when she happened to see him chewing on an electric cord. "You'll fry like rice," she screamed. The only people around were Don and one of Sue Ann's macrobiotic friends and somebody who was on his way to a commune in the Santa Lucias, and they didn't notice Sue Ann screaming at Michael because they were in the kitchen trying to retrieve some very good Moroccan hash which had dropped down through a floorboard damaged in the fire.

1967

II
PERSONALS

On Keeping a Notebook

"'THAT WOMAN ESTELLE,'" the note reads, "'is partly the reason why George Sharp and I are separated today.' *Dirty crepe-de-Chine wrapper, hotel bar, Wilmington RR, 9:45 a.m. August Monday morning.*"

Since the note is in my notebook, it presumably has some meaning to me. I study it for a long while. At first I have only the most general notion of what I was doing on an August Monday morning in the bar of the hotel across from the Pennsylvania Railroad station in Wilmington, Delaware (waiting for a train? missing one? 1960? 1961? why Wilmington?), but I do remember being there. The woman in the dirty crepe-de-Chine wrapper had come down from her room for a beer, and the bartender had heard before the reason why George Sharp and she were separated today. "Sure," he said, and went on mopping the floor. "You told me." At the other end of the bar

192 | JOAN DIDION

is a girl. She is talking, pointedly, not to the man beside her but to a cat lying in the triangle of sunlight cast through the open door. She is wearing a plaid silk dress from Peck & Peck, and the hem is coming down.

Here is what it is: the girl has been on the Eastern Shore, and now she is going back to the city, leaving the man beside her, and all she can see ahead are the viscous summer sidewalks and the 3 a.m. long-distance calls that will make her lie awake and then sleep drugged through all the steaming mornings left in August (1960? 1961?). Because she must go directly from the train to lunch in New York, she wishes that she had a safety pin for the hem of the plaid silk dress, and she also wishes that she could forget about the hem and the lunch and stay in the cool bar that smells of disinfectant and malt and make friends with the woman in the crepe-de-Chine wrapper. She is afflicted by a little self-pity, and she wants to compare Estelles. That is what that was all about.

Why did I write it down? In order to remember, of course, but exactly what was it I wanted to remember? How much of it actually happened? Did any of it? Why do I keep a notebook at all? It is easy to deceive oneself on all those scores. The impulse to write things down is a peculiarly compulsive one, inexplicable to those who do not share it, useful only accidentally, only secondarily, in the way that any compulsion tries to justify itself. I suppose that it begins or does not begin in the cradle. Although I have felt compelled to write things down since I was five years old, I doubt that my daughter ever will, for she is a singularly blessed and accepting child, delighted with life exactly as life presents itself to her, unafraid to go to sleep and unafraid to wake up. Keepers of private notebooks are a different breed altogether, lonely and resistant rearrangers of things, anxious malcontents, children afflicted apparently at birth with some presentiment of loss.

My first notebook was a Big Five tablet, given to me by my mother with the sensible suggestion that I stop whining and learn to amuse myself by writing down my thoughts. She returned the tablet to me a few years ago; the first entry is an account of a woman who believed herself to be freezing to death in the Arctic night, only to find, when day broke, that she had stumbled onto the Sahara Desert, where she would die of the heat before lunch. I have no idea what turn of a five-year-old's mind could have prompted so insistently "ironic" and exotic a story, but it does reveal a certain predilection for the extreme which has dogged me into adult life; perhaps if I were analytically inclined I would find it a truer story than any I might have told about Donald Johnson's birthday party or the day my cousin Brenda put Kitty Litter in the aquarium.

So the point of my keeping a notebook has never been, nor is it now, to have an accurate factual record of what I have been doing or thinking. That would be a different impulse entirely, an instinct for reality which I sometimes envy but do not possess. At no point have I ever been able successfully to keep a diary; my approach to daily life ranges from the grossly negligent to the merely absent, and on those few occasions when I have tried dutifully to record a day's events, boredom has so overcome me that the results are mysterious at best. What is this business about "shopping, typing piece, dinner with E, depressed"? Shopping for what? Typing what piece? Who is E? Was this "E" depressed, or was I depressed? Who cares?

In fact I have abandoned altogether that kind of pointless entry; instead I tell what some would call lies. "That's simply not true," the members of my family frequently tell me when they come up against my memory of a shared event. "The party was *not* for you, the spider was *not* a black widow, *it wasn't that way at all*." Very likely they are right, for not only have I always had trouble distinguishing between what happened and what merely might have happened, but I remain unconvinced that the distinction, for my purposes, matters. The cracked crab that I recall having for lunch the day my father came home from Detroit in 1945 must certainly be embroidery, worked into the day's pattern to lend verisimilitude;

I was ten years old and would not now remember the cracked crab. The day's events did not turn on cracked crab. And yet it is precisely that fictitious crab that makes me see the afternoon all over again, a home movie run all too often, the father bearing gifts, the child weeping, an exercise in family love and guilt. Or that is what it was to me. Similarly, perhaps it never did snow that August in Vermont; perhaps there never were flurries in the night wind, and maybe no one else felt the ground hardening and summer already dead even as we pretended to bask in it, but that was how it felt to me, and it might as well have snowed, could have snowed, did snow.

How it felt to me: that is getting closer to the truth about a notebook. I sometimes delude myself about why I keep a notebook, imagine that some thrifty virtue derives from preserving everything observed. See enough and write it down, I tell myself, and then some morning when the world seems drained of wonder, some day when I am only going through the motions of doing what I am supposed to do, which is write—

on that bankrupt morning I will simply
open my notebook and there it will all be, a
forgotten account with accumulated interest, paid passage back to the world out there:
dialogue overheard in hotels and elevators
and at the hatcheck counter in Pavillon (one
middle-aged man shows his hat check to another and says, "That's my old football number"); impressions of Bettina Aptheker and
Benjamin Sonnenberg and Teddy ("Mr. Acapulco") Stauffer; careful *aperçus* about tennis
bums and failed fashion models and Greek
shipping heiresses, one of whom taught me
a significant lesson (a lesson I could have
learned from F. Scott Fitzgerald, but perhaps we all must meet the very rich for ourselves) by asking, when I arrived to interview
her in her orchid-filled sitting room on the
second day of a paralyzing New York bliz-
zard, whether it was snowing outside.

I imagine, in other words, that the notebook is about other people. But of course it
is not. I have no real business with what one
stranger said to another at the hat-check
counter in Pavillon; in fact I suspect that
the line "That's my old football number"

touched not my own imagination at all, but merely some memory of something once read, probably "The Eighty-Yard Run." Nor is my concern with a woman in a dirty crepe-de-Chine wrapper in a Wilmington bar. My stake is always, of course, in the unmentioned girl in the plaid silk dress. *Remember what it was to be me*: that is always the point.

It is a difficult point to admit. We are brought up in the ethic that others, any others, all others, are by definition more interesting than ourselves; taught to be diffident, just this side of self-effacing. ("You're the least important person in the room and don't forget it," Jessica Mitford's governess would hiss in her ear on the advent of any social occasion; I copied that into my notebook because it is only recently that I have been able to enter a room without hearing some such phrase in my inner ear.) Only the very young and the very old may recount their dreams at breakfast, dwell upon self, interrupt with memories of beach picnics and favorite Liberty lawn dresses and the rainbow trout in a creek near Colorado Springs. The rest of us are expected, rightly, to affect absorption in other people's favorite dresses, other people's trout.

And so we do. But our notebooks give us away, for however dutifully we record what we see around us, the common denominator of all we see is always, transparently, shamelessly, the implacable "I." We are not talking here about the kind of notebook that is patently for public consumption, a structural conceit for binding together a series of graceful *pensées*; we are talking about something private, about bits of the mind's string too short to use, an indiscriminate and erratic assemblage with meaning only for its maker.

And sometimes even the maker has difficulty with the meaning. There does not seem to be, for example, any point in my knowing for the rest of my life that, during 1964, 720 tons of soot fell on every square mile of New York City, yet there it is in my notebook, labeled "FACT." Nor do I really need to remember that Ambrose Bierce liked to spell Leland Stanford's name "£eland $tanford" or that "smart women almost always wear black in Cuba," a fashion hint without much potential for practical application. And does not the relevance of these notes seem marginal at best?:

> In the basement museum of the Inyo County Courthouse in Independence, California, sign pinned to a mandarin coat: "This MANDARIN COAT was often worn by Mrs. Minnie S. Brooks when giving lectures on her TEAPOT COLLECTION."

> Redhead getting out of car in front of Beverly Wilshire Hotel, chinchilla stole, Vuitton bags with tags reading:

> MRS LOU FOX
> HOTEL SAHARA
> VEGAS

Well, perhaps not entirely marginal. As a matter of fact, Mrs. Minnie S. Brooks and her MANDARIN COAT pull me back into my

own childhood, for although I never knew
Mrs. Brooks and did not visit Inyo County
until I was thirty, I grew up in just such a
world, in houses cluttered with Indian rel-
ics and bits of gold ore and ambergris and
the souvenirs my Aunt Mercy Farnsworth
brought back from the Orient. It is a long
way from that world to Mrs. Lou Fox's
world, where we all live now, and is it not
just as well to remember that? Might not
Mrs. Minnie S. Brooks help me to remember what I am? Might not Mrs. Lou Fox
help me to remember what I am not?

But sometimes the point is harder to discern. What exactly did I have in mind
when I noted down that it cost the father of
someone I know $650 a month to light the
place on the Hudson in which he lived before the Crash? What use was I planning to
make of this line by Jimmy Hoffa: "I may
have my faults, but being wrong ain't one of
them"? And although I think it interesting
to know where the girls who travel with the

Syndicate have their hair done when they find themselves on the West Coast, will I ever make suitable use of it? Might I not be better off just passing it on to John O'Hara? What is a recipe for sauerkraut doing in my notebook? What kind of magpie keeps this notebook? *"He was born the night the Titanic went down."* That seems a nice enough line, and I even recall who said it, but is it not really a better line in life than it could ever be in fiction?

But of course that is exactly it: not that I should ever use the line, but that I should remember the woman who said it and the afternoon I heard it. We were on her terrace by the sea, and we were finishing the wine left from lunch, trying to get what sun there was, a California winter sun. The woman whose husband was born the night the *Titanic* went down wanted to rent her house, wanted to go back to her children in Paris. I remember wishing that I could afford the house, which cost $1,000 a month. "Some-day you will," she said lazily. "Someday it all comes." There in the sun on her terrace it seemed easy to believe in someday, but later

I had a low-grade afternoon hangover and ran over a black snake on the way to the supermarket and was flooded with inexplicable fear when I heard the checkout clerk explaining to the man ahead of me why she was finally divorcing her husband. "He left me no choice," she said over and over as she punched the register. "He has a little seven-month-old baby by her, he left me no choice." I would like to believe that my dread then was for the human condition, but of course it was for me, because I wanted a baby and did not then have one and because I wanted to own the house that cost $1,000 a month to rent and because I had a hangover.

It all comes back. Perhaps it is difficult to see the value in having one's self back in that kind of mood, but I do see it; I think we are well advised to keep on nodding terms with the people we used to be, whether we find them attractive company or not. Otherwise they turn up unannounced and surprise us, come hammering on the mind's door at 4 a.m. of a bad night and demand to know who deserted them, who betrayed them, who is going to make amends. We forget all too soon the things we thought we could never forget. We forget the loves and the betrayals alike, forget what we whispered and what we screamed, forget who we were. I have already lost touch with a couple of people I used to be; one of them, a seventeen-year-old, presents little threat, although it would be of some interest to me to know again what it feels like to sit on a river levee drinking vodka-and-orange-juice and listening to Les Paul and Mary Ford and their echoes sing "How High the Moon" on the car radio. (You see I still have the scenes, but I no longer perceive myself among those present, no longer could even improvise the dialogue.) The other one, a twenty-three-year-old, bothers me more. She was always a good deal of trouble, and I suspect she will reappear when I least want to see her, skirts too long, shy to the point of aggravation, always the injured party, full of recriminations and little hurts and stories I do not want to hear again, at once saddening me and angering me with her vulnerability and ignorance, an apparition all the more insistent for being so long banished.

It is a good idea, then, to keep in touch, and I suppose that keeping in touch is what notebooks are all about. And we are all on our own when it comes to keeping those lines open to ourselves: your notebook will never help me, nor mine you. *"So what's new in the whiskey business?"* What could that possibly mean to you? To me it means a blonde in a Pucci bathing suit sitting with a couple of fat men by the pool at the Beverly Hills Hotel. Another man approaches, and they all regard one another in silence for a while. "So what's new in the whiskey business?" one of the fat men finally says by way of welcome, and the blonde stands up, arches one foot and dips it in the pool, looking all the while at the cabaña where Baby Pignatari is talking on the telephone. That is all there is to that, except that several years later I saw the blonde coming out of Saks Fifth Avenue in New York with her California complexion and a voluminous mink coat. In the harsh wind that day she looked old and irrevocably tired to me, and even the skins in the mink coat were not worked the way they were doing them that year, not the way she would have wanted them done, and there is the point of the story. For a while after that I did not like to look in the mirror, and my eyes would skim the newspapers and pick out only the deaths, the cancer victims, the premature coronaries, the suicides, and I stopped riding the Lexington Avenue IRT because I noticed for the first time that all the strangers I had seen for years—the man with the seeing-eye dog, the spinster who read the classified pages every day, the fat girl who always got off with me at Grand Central—looked older than they once had.

It all comes back. Even that recipe for sauerkraut: even that brings it back. I was on Fire Island when I first made that sauerkraut, and it was raining, and we drank a lot of bourbon and ate the sauerkraut and went to bed at ten, and I listened to the rain and the Atlantic and felt safe. I made the sauerkraut again last night and it did not make me feel any safer, but that is, as they say, another story.

1966

On Self-Respect

ONCE, IN A DRY SEASON, I wrote in large letters across two pages of a notebook that innocence ends when one is stripped of the delusion that one likes oneself. Although now, some years later, I marvel that a mind on the outs with itself should have nonetheless made painstaking record of its every tremor, I recall with embarrassing clarity the flavor of those particular ashes. It was a matter of misplaced self-respect.

I had not been elected to Phi Beta Kappa. This failure could scarcely have been more predictable or less ambiguous (I simply did not have the grades), but I was unnerved by it; I had somehow thought myself a kind of academic Raskolnikov, curiously exempt from the cause-effect relationships which hampered others. Although even the humorless nineteen-year-old that I was must have recognized that the situation lacked real tragic stature, the day that I did not

make Phi Beta Kappa nonetheless marked
the end of something, and innocence may
well be the word for it. I lost the conviction
that lights would always turn green for me,
the pleasant certainty that those rather pas-
sive virtues which had won me approval as
a child automatically guaranteed me not
only Phi Beta Kappa keys but happiness,
honor, and the love of a good man; lost a certain touching faith in the totem power of
good manners, clean hair, and proven competence on the Stanford-Binet scale. To
such doubtful amulets had my self respect
been pinned, and I faced myself that day
with the nonplused apprehension of someone who has come across a vampire and has
no crucifix at hand.

Although to be driven back upon oneself
is an uneasy affair at best, rather like trying to cross a border with borrowed creden-
tials, it seems to me now the one condition
necessary to the beginnings of real self-
respect. Most of our platitudes notwithstanding, self-deception remains the most
difficult deception. The tricks that work on
others count for nothing in that very well-

lit back alley where one keeps assignations with oneself: no winning smiles will do here, no prettily drawn lists of good intentions. One shuffles flashily but in vain through one's marked cards—the kindness done for the wrong reason, the apparent triumph which involved no real effort, the seemingly heroic act into which one had been shamed. The dismal fact is that self-respect has nothing to do with the approval of others—who are, after all, deceived easily enough; has nothing to do with reputation, which, as Rhett Butler told Scarlett O'Hara, is something people with courage can do without.

To do without self-respect, on the other hand, is to be an unwilling audience of one to an interminable documentary that details one's failings, both real and imagined, with fresh footage spliced in for every screening. *There's the glass you broke in anger, there's the hurt on X's face; watch now, this next scene, the night Y came back from Houston, see how you muff this one.* To live without self-respect is to live awake some night, beyond the reach of warm milk, phenobarbital, and the sleeping hand on the coverlet, counting up the sins of commission and omission, the trusts betrayed, the promises subtly broken, the gifts irrevocably wasted through sloth or cowardice or carelessness. However long we postpone it, we eventually lie down alone in that notoriously uncomfortable bed, the one we make ourselves. Whether or not we sleep in it depends, of course, on whether or not we respect ourselves.

To protest that some fairly improbable people, some people who *could not possibly respect themselves*, seem to sleep easily enough is to miss the point entirely, as surely as those people miss it who think that self-respect has necessarily to do with not having safety pins in one's underwear. There is a common superstition that "self-respect" is a kind of charm against snakes, something that keeps those who have it locked in some unblighted Eden, out of strange beds, ambivalent conversations, and trouble in general. It does not at all. It has nothing to do with the face of things, but concerns instead a separate peace, a private reconciliation. Although the careless, suicidal Julian English in *Appointment in Samarra* and the careless, incurably dishonest Jordan Baker in *The Great Gatsby* seem equally improbable candidates for self-respect, Jordan Baker had it, Julian English did not. With that genius for accommodation more often seen in women than in men, Jordan took her own measure, made her own peace, avoided threats to that peace: "I hate careless people," she told Nick Carraway. "It takes two to make an accident."

Like Jordan Baker, people with self-respect have the courage of their mistakes. They know the price of things. If they choose to commit adultery, they do not then go running, in an access of bad conscience, to receive absolution from the wronged parties; nor do they complain unduly of the unfairness, the undeserved embarrassment, of being named co-respondent. In brief, people with self-respect exhibit a certain toughness, a kind of moral nerve; they display what was once called *character*, a quality which, although approved in the abstract, sometimes loses ground to other, more instantly negotiable virtues. The measure of its slipping prestige is that one tends to think of it only in connection with homely children and United States senators who have been defeated, preferably in the primary, for reelection. Nonetheless, character—the willingness to accept responsibility for one's own life—is the source from which self-respect springs.

Self-respect is something that our grandparents, whether or not they had it, knew all about. They had instilled in them, young, a certain discipline, the sense that one lives by doing things one does not particularly want to do, by putting fears and doubts to one side, by weighing immediate comforts against the possibility of larger, even intangible, comforts. It seemed to the nineteenth century admirable, but not remarkable, that Chinese Gordon put on a clean white suit and held Khartoum against the Mahdi; it did not seem unjust that the way to free land in California involved death and difficulty and dirt. In a diary kept during the winter of 1846, an emigrating twelve-year-old named Narcissa Cornwall noted coolly: "Father was busy reading and did not notice that the house was being filled with strange Indians until Mother spoke about it." Even lacking any clue as to what Mother said, one can scarcely fail to be impressed by the entire incident: the father reading, the Indians filing in, the mother choosing the words that would not alarm, the child duly recording the event and noting further that those particular Indians were not, "fortunately for us," hostile. Indians were simply part of the *donnée*.

In one guise or another, Indians always are. Again, it is a question of recognizing that anything worth having has its price. People who respect themselves are willing to accept the risk that the Indians will be hostile, that the venture will go bankrupt, that the liaison may not turn out to be one in which *every day is a holiday because you're married to me*. They are willing to invest something of themselves; they may not play at all, but when they do play, they know the odds.

That kind of self-respect is a discipline, a habit of mind that can never be faked but can be developed, trained, coaxed forth. It was once suggested to me that, as an antidote to crying, I put my head in a paper bag. As it happens, there is a sound physiological reason, something to do with oxygen, for doing exactly that, but the psychological effect alone is incalculable: it is difficult in the extreme to continue fancying oneself Cathy in *Wuthering Heights* with one's head in a Food Fair bag. There is a similar case for all the small disciplines, unimportant in themselves; imagine maintaining any kind of swoon, commiserative or carnal, in a cold shower.

But those small disciplines are valuable only insofar as they represent larger ones. To say that Waterloo was won on the playing fields of Eton is not to say that Napoleon might have been saved by a crash program in cricket; to give formal dinners in the rain forest would be pointless did not the candlelight flickering on the liana call forth deeper, stronger disciplines, values instilled long before. It is a kind of ritual, helping us to remember who and what we are. In order to remember it, one must have known it.

To have that sense of one's intrinsic worth which constitutes self-respect is potentially to have everything: the ability to discriminate, to love and to remain indifferent. To lack it is to be locked within oneself, paradoxically incapable of either love or indifference. If we do not respect ourselves, we are on the one hand forced to despise those who have so few resources as to consort with us, so little perception as to remain blind to our fatal weaknesses. On the other, we are peculiarly in thrall to everyone we see, curiously determined to live out—since our self-image is untenable—their false notions of us. We flatter ourselves by thinking this compulsion to please others an attractive trait: a gist for imaginative empathy, evidence of our willingness to give. Of *course* I will play Francesca to your Paolo, Helen Keller to anyone's Annie Sullivan: no expectation is too misplaced, no role too ludicrous. At the mercy of those we cannot but hold in contempt, we play roles doomed to failure before they are begun, each defeat generating fresh despair at the urgency of divining and meeting the next demand made upon us.

It is the phenomenon sometimes called "alienation from self." In its advanced stages, we no longer answer the telephone, because someone might want something; that we could say *no* without drowning in self-reproach is an idea alien to this game. Every encounter demands too much, tears the nerves, drains the will, and the specter of something as small as an unanswered letter arouses such disproportionate guilt that answering it becomes out of the question. To assign unanswered letters their proper weight, to free us from the expectations of others, to give us back to ourselves—there lies the great, the singular power of self-respect. Without it, one eventually discovers the final turn of the screw: one runs away to find oneself, and finds no one at home.

1961

I Can't Get That Monster out of My Mind

QUITE EARLY in the action of an otherwise
unmemorable monster movie (I do not even
remember its name), having to do with a
mechanical man who walks underwater
down the East River as far as Forty-ninth
Street and then surfaces to destroy the
United Nations, the heroine is surveying
the grounds of her country place when the
mechanical monster bobs up from a lake
and attempts to carry off her child. (Actually we are aware that the monster wants
only to make friends with the little girl, but
the young mother, who has presumably seen
fewer monster movies than we have, is not.
This provides pathos, and dramatic tension.) Later that evening, as the heroine
sits on the veranda reflecting upon the day's
events, her brother strolls out, tamps his
pipe, and asks: "Why the brown study,
Deborah?" Deborah smiles, ruefully. "It's

nothing, Jim, really," she says. "I just can't get that monster out of my mind."

I just can't get that monster out of my mind. It is a useful line, and one that frequently occurs to me when I catch the tone in which a great many people write or talk about Hollywood. In the popular imagination, the American motion-picture industry still represents a kind of mechanical monster, programmed to stifle and destroy all that is interesting and worthwhile and "creative" in the human spirit. As an adjective, the very word "Hollywood" has long been pejorative and suggestive of something referred to as "the System," a phrase delivered with the same sinister emphasis that James Cagney once lent to "the Syndicate." The System not only strangles talent but poisons the soul, a fact supported by rich webs of lore. Mention Hollywood, and we are keyed to remember Scott Fitzgerald, dying at Malibu, attended only by Sheilah Graham while he ground out college-weekend movies (he was also writing *The Last Tycoon*, but that is not part of the story); we are conditioned to recall the brightest minds of a generation, deteriorat-

ing around the swimming pool at the Garden of Allah while they waited for calls
from the Thalberg Building. (Actually it
takes a fairly romantic sensibility to discern
why the Garden of Allah should have been
a more insidious ambiance than the Algon-
quin, or why the Thalberg Building, and
Metro-Goldwyn-Mayer, should have been
more morally debilitating than the Graybar
Building, and *Vanity Fair*. Edmund Wilson,
who has this kind of sensibility, once suggested that it has something to do with the
weather. Perhaps it does.)

Hollywood the Destroyer. It was essentially a romantic vision, and before long
Hollywood was helping actively to perpet-
uate it: think of Jack Palance, as a movie star
finally murdered by the System in *The Big
Knife*; think of Judy Garland and James Ma-
son (and of Janet Gaynor and Fredric
March before them), their lives blighted
by the System, or by the Studio—the two
phrases were, when the old major studios
still ran Hollywood, more or less inter-
changeable—in *A Star Is Born*. By now, the
corruption and venality and restrictiveness

of Hollywood have become such firm tenets of American social faith—and of Hollywood's own image of itself—that I was only mildly surprised, not long ago, to hear a young screenwriter announce that Hollywood was "ruining" him. "As a writer," he added. "As a writer," he had previously written, over a span of ten years in New York, one comedy (as opposed to "comic") novel, several newspaper reviews of other people's comedy novels, and a few years' worth of captions for a picture magazine.

Now. It is not surprising that the specter of Hollywood the Destroyer still haunts the rote middle intelligentsia (the monster lurks, I understand, in the wilds between the Thalia and the Museum of Modern Art), or at least those members of it who have not yet perceived the *chic* conferred upon Hollywood by the *Cahiers du Cinéma* set. (Those who have perceived it adopt an equally extreme position, speculating endlessly about what Vincente Minelli was up to in *Meet Me in St. Louis*, attending seminars on Nicholas Ray, that kind of thing.) What is surprising is that the monster still haunts Hollywood itself—and Hollywood knows better, knows that the monster was laid to rest, dead of natural causes, some years ago. The Fox back lot is now a complex of office buildings called Century City; Paramount makes not forty movies a year but "Bonanza." What was once The Studio is now a releasing operation, and even the Garden of Allah is no more. Virtually every movie made is an independent production— and is that not what we once wanted? Is that not what we once said could revolutionize American movies? The millennium is here, the era of "fewer and better" motion pictures, and what have we? We have fewer pictures, but not necessarily better pictures. Ask Hollywood why, and Hollywood resorts to murmuring about the monster. It has been, they say, impossible to work "honestly" in Hollywood. Certain things have prevented it. The studios, or what is left of the studios, thwart their every dream. The moneymen conspire against them. New York spirits away their prints before they have finished cutting. They are bound by clichés. There is something wrong with "the intellectual climate." If only they were allowed some freedom, if only they could exercise an individual voice. . . .

If only. These protests have about them an engaging period optimism, depending as they do upon the Rousseauean premise that most people, left to their own devices, think not in clichés but with originality and brilliance; that most individual voices, once heard, turn out to be voices of beauty and wisdom. I think we would all agree that a novel is nothing if it is not the expression of an individual voice, of a single view of experience—and how many good or even interesting novels, of the thousands published, appear each year? I doubt that more can be expected of the motion-picture industry. Men who do have interesting individual voices have for some time now been making movies in which those voices are heard; I think of Elia Kazan's *America America*, and, with a good deal less enthusiasm for the voice, of Stanley Kubrick's *Dr. Strangelove*.

But it is not only the "interesting" voices who now have the opportunity to be heard.

John Frankenheimer was quoted in *Life* as admitting: "You can't call Hollywood 'The Industry' any more. Today we have a chance to put our personal fantasies on film." Frankenheimer's own personal fantasies have included *All Fall Down*, in which we learned that Warren Beatty and Eva Marie Saint were in love when Frankenheimer dissolved to some swans shimmering on a lake, and *Seven Days in May*, which, in its misapprehension of the way the American power elite thinks and talks and operates (the movie's United States Senator from California, as I recall, drove a Rolls-Royce), appeared to be fantasy in the most clinical sense of that word. Carl Foreman, who, before he was given a chance to put his personal fantasies on film, worked on some very good (of their type) movies—*High Noon* and *The Guns of Navarone*, for two—later released what he called his "personal statement": *The Victors*, a phenomenon which suggests only that two heads are perhaps better than one, if that one is Foreman's.

One problem is that American directors, with a handful of exceptions, are not much interested in style; they are at heart didactic. Ask what they plan to do with their absolute freedom, with their chance to make a personal statement, and they will pick an "issue," a "problem." The "issues" they pick are generally no longer real issues, if indeed they ever were—but I think it a mistake to attribute this to any calculated venality, to any conscious playing it safe. (I am reminded of a screenwriter who just recently discovered dwarfs—although he, like the rest of us, must have lived through that period when dwarfs turned up on the fiction pages of the glossier magazines with the approximate frequency that Suzy Parker turned up on the advertising pages. This screenwriter sees dwarfs as symbols of modern man's crippling anomie. There is a certain cultural lag.) Call it instead—this apparent calculation about what "issues" are now safe—an absence of imagination, a sloppiness of mind in some ways encouraged by a comfortable feedback from the audience, from the bulk of the reviewers, and from some people who ought to know better. Stanley Kramer's *Judgment at Nuremberg,* made in 1961, was an intrepid indictment not of authoritarianism in the abstract, not of the trials themselves, not of the various moral and legal issues involved, but of Nazi war atrocities, about which there would have seemed already to be some consensus. (You may remember that *Judgment at Nuremberg* received an Academy Award, which the screenwriter Abby Mann accepted on the behalf of "all intellectuals.") Later, Kramer and Abby Mann collaborated on *Ship of Fools*, into which they injected "a little more compassion and humor" and in which they advanced the action from 1931 to 1933—the better to register another defiant protest against the National Socialist Party. Foreman's *The Victors* set forth, interminably, the proposition that war defeats the victors equally with the vanquished, a notion not exactly radical. (Foreman is a director who at first gives the impression of having a little style, but the impression is entirely spurious, and prompted mostly by his total recall for old Eisenstein effects.) Stanley Kubrick's *Dr. Strangelove*, which did have a little style, was scarcely a picture of relentless originality; rarely have we seen so much made over so little. John Simon, in the *New Leader*, declared that the "altogether admirable thing" about *Dr. Strangelove* was that it managed to be "thoroughly irreverent about everything the Establishment takes seriously: atomic war, government, the army, international relations, heroism, sex, and what not." I don't know who John Simon thinks makes up the Establishment, but skimming back at random from "what not," sex is our most durable communal joke; Billy Wilder's *One, Two, Three* was a boffo (*cf. Variety*) spoof of international relations; the army as a laugh line has filtered right down to Phil Silvers and "Sergeant Bilko"; and, if "government" is something about which the American Establishment is inflexibly reverent, I seem to have been catching some pretty underground material on prime time television. And what not. *Dr. Strangelove* was essentially a one-line gag, having to do with the difference between all other wars and nuclear war. By the time George Scott had said "I think I'll

mosey on over to the War Room" and
Sterling Hayden had said "Looks like we
got ourselves a shootin' war" and the SAC
bomber had begun heading for its Soviet
targets to the tune of "When Johnny Comes
Marching Home Again," Kubrick had already developed a full fugue upon the
theme, and should have started counting the
minutes until it would begin to pall.

What we have, then, are a few interesting minds at work; and a great many less interesting ones. The European situation is
not all that different. Antonioni, among the
Italians, makes beautiful, intelligent, intri-
cately and subtly built pictures, the power
of which lies entirely in their structure; Vis-
conti, on the other hand, has less sense of
form than anyone now directing. One might
as well have viewed a series of stills, in no
perceptible order, as his *The Leopard*. Fed-
erico Fellini and Ingmar Bergman share
a stunning visual intelligence and a numbingly banal view of human experience;
Alain Resnais, in *Last Year at Marienbad*
and *Muriel*, demonstrated a style so intrusive

that one suspected it to be a smoke screen, suspected that it was intruding upon a vacuum. As for the notion that European movies tend to be more original than American movies, no one who saw *Boccaccio '70* could ever again automatically modify the word "formula" with "Hollywood."

So. With perhaps a little prodding from abroad, we are all grown up now in Hollywood, and left to set out in the world on our own. We are no longer in the grip of a monster; Harry Cohn no longer runs Columbia like, as the saying went, a concentration camp. Whether or not a picture receives a Code seal no longer matters much at the box office. No more curfew, no more Daddy, *anything goes*. Some of us do not quite like this permissiveness; some of us would like to find "reasons" why our pictures are not as good as we know in our hearts they might be. Not long ago I met a producer who complained to me of the difficulties he had working within what I recognized as the

System, although he did not call it that. He longed, he said, to do an adaptation of a certain Charles Jackson short story. "Some really terrific stuff," he said. "Can't touch it, I'm afraid. About masturbation."

1964

On Morality

As it happens I am in Death Valley, in a room at the Enterprise Motel and Trailer Park, and it is July, and it is hot. In fact it is 119°. I cannot seem to make the air conditioner work, but there is a small refrigerator, and I can wrap ice cubes in a towel and hold them against the small of my back. With the help of the ice cubes I have been trying to think, because *The American Scholar* asked me to, in some abstract way about "morality," a word I distrust more every day, but my mind veers inflexibly toward the particular.

Here are some particulars. At midnight last night, on the road in from Las Vegas to Death Valley Junction, a car hit a shoulder and turned over. The driver, very young and apparently drunk, was killed instantly. His girl was found alive but bleeding internally, deep in shock. I talked this afternoon to the nurse who had driven the girl to the nearest doctor, 185 miles across the floor of the Valley and three ranges of lethal mountain road. The nurse explained that her husband, a talc miner, had stayed on the highway with the boy's body until the coroner could get over the mountains from Bishop, at dawn today. "You can't just leave a body on the highway," she said. "It's immoral."

It was one instance in which I did not distrust the word, because she meant something quite specific. She meant that if a body is left alone for even a few minutes on the desert, the coyotes close in and eat the flesh. Whether or not a corpse is torn apart by coyotes may seem only a sentimental consideration, but of course it is more: one of the promises we make to one another is that we will try to retrieve our casualties, try not to abandon our dead to the coyotes. If we have been taught to keep our promises—if, in the simplest terms, our upbringing is good enough—we stay with the body, or have bad dreams.

I am talking, of course, about the kind of social code that is sometimes called, usually pejoratively, "wagon-train morality." In fact that is precisely what it is. For better or worse, we are what we learned as children: my own childhood was illuminated by graphic litanies of the grief awaiting those who failed in their loyalties to each other. The Donner-Reed Party, starving in the Sierra snows, all the ephemera of civilization gone save that one vestigial taboo, the provision that no one should eat his own blood kin. The Jayhawkers, who quarreled and separated not far from where I am tonight. Some of them died in the Funerals and some of them died down near Badwater and most of the rest of them died in the Panamints. A woman who got through gave the Valley its name. Some might say that the Jayhawkers were killed by the desert summer, and the Donner Party by the mountain winter, by circumstances beyond control; we were taught instead that they had somewhere abdicated their responsibilities, somehow breached their primary loyalties, or they would not have found themselves helpless in the mountain winter or the desert summer, would not have given way to acrimony, would not have deserted one another, would not have *failed*. In brief, we heard such stories as cautionary tales, and they still suggest the only kind of "morality" that seems to me to have any but the most potentially mendacious meaning.

You are quite possibly impatient with me by now; I am talking, you want to say, about a "morality" so primitive that it scarcely deserves the name, a code that has as its point only survival, not the attainment of the ideal good. Exactly. Particularly out here tonight, in this country so ominous and terrible that to live in it is to live with antimatter, it is difficult to believe that "the good" is a knowable quantity. Let me tell you what it is like out here tonight. Stories travel at night on the desert. Someone gets in his pickup and drives a couple of hundred miles for a beer, and he carries news of what is happening, back wherever he came from. Then he drives another hundred miles for another beer, and passes along stories from the last place as well as from the one before; it is a

234 | JOAN DIDION

network kept alive by people whose instincts tell them that if they do not keep moving at night on the desert they will lose all reason. Here is a story that is going around the desert tonight: over across the Nevada line, sheriff's deputies are diving in some underground pools, trying to retrieve a couple of bodies known to be in the hole. The widow of one of the drowned boys is over there; she is eighteen, and pregnant, and is said not to leave the hole. The divers go down and come up, and she just stands there and stares into the water. They have been diving for ten days but have found no bottom to the caves, no bodies and no trace of them, only the black 90° water going down and down and down, and a single translucent fish, not classified. The story tonight is that one of the divers has been hauled up incoherent, out of his head, shouting—until they got him out of there so that the widow could not hear—about water that got hotter instead of cooler as he went down, about light flickering through the water, about magma, about underground nuclear testing.

That is the tone stories take out here, and there are quite a few of them tonight. And it is more than the stories alone. Across the road at the Faith Community Church a couple of dozen old people, come here to live in trailers and die in the sun, are holding a prayer sing. I cannot hear them and do not want to. What I can hear are occasional coyotes and a constant chorus of "Baby the Rain Must Fall" from the jukebox in the Snake Room next door, and if I were also to hear those dying voices, those Midwestern voices drawn to this lunar country for some unimaginable atavistic rites, *rock of ages cleft for me*, I think I would lose my own reason. Every now and then I imagine I hear a rattlesnake, but my husband says that it is a faucet, a paper rustling, the wind. Then he stands by a window, and plays a flashlight over the dry wash outside.

What does it mean? It means nothing manageable. There is some sinister hysteria in the air out here tonight, some hint of the monstrous perversion to which any human idea can come. "I followed my own conscience." "I did what I thought was right." How many madmen have said it and meant it? How many murderers? Klaus Fuchs said it, and the men who committed the Mountain Meadows Massacre said it, and Alfred Rosenberg said it. And, as we are rotely and rather presumptuously reminded by those who would say it now, Jesus said it. Maybe we have all said it, and maybe we have been wrong. Except on that most primitive level—our loyalties to those we love—what could be more arrogant than to claim the primacy of personal conscience? ("Tell me," a rabbi asked Daniel Bell when he said, as a child, that he did not believe in God. "Do you think God cares?") At least some of the time, the world appears to me as a painting by Hieronymous Bosch; were I to follow my conscience then, it would lead me out onto the desert with Marion Faye, out to where he stood in *The Deer Park* looking east to Los Alamos and praying, as if for rain, that it would happen: "*. . . let it come and clear the rot and the stench and the stink, let it come for all of everywhere, just so it comes and the world stands clear in the white dead dawn.*"

Of course you will say that I do not have the right, even if I had the power, to inflict that unreasonable conscience upon you; nor do I want you to inflict your conscience, however reasonable, however enlightened, upon me. ("We must be aware of the dangers which lie in our most generous wishes," Lionel Trilling once wrote. "Some paradox of our nature leads us, when once we have made our fellow men the objects of our enlightened interest, to go on to make them the objects of our pity, then of our wisdom, ultimately of our coercion.") That the ethic of conscience is intrinsically insidious seems scarcely a revelatory point, but it is one raised with increasing infrequency; even those who do raise it tend to *segue* with troubling readiness into the quite contradictory position that the ethic of conscience is dangerous when it is "wrong," and admirable when it is "right."

You see I want to be quite obstinate about insisting that we have no way of knowing—beyond that fundamental loyalty to the social code—what is "right" and what is "wrong," what is "good" and what "evil." I dwell so upon this because the most disturbing aspect of "morality" seems to me to be the frequency with which the word now appears; in the press, on television, in the most perfunctory kinds of conversation. Questions of straightforward power (or survival) politics, questions of quite indifferent public policy, questions of almost anything: they are all assigned these factitious moral burdens. There is something facile going on, some self-indulgence at work. Of course we would all like to "believe" in something, like to assuage our private guilts in public causes, like to lose our tiresome selves; like, perhaps, to transform the white flag of defeat at home into the brave white banner of battle away from home. And of course it is all right to do that; that is how, immemorially, things have gotten done. But I think it is all right only so long as we do not delude ourselves about what we are doing, and why. It is all right only so long as we remember that all the *ad hoc* committees, all the picket lines, all the brave signatures in *The New York Times*, all the tools of agitprop straight across the spectrum, do not confer upon anyone any *ipso facto* virtue. It is all right only so long as we recognize that the end may or may not be expedient, may or may not be a good idea, but in any case has nothing to do with "morality." Because when we start deceiving ourselves into thinking not that we want something or need something, not that it is a pragmatic necessity for us to have it, but that it is a *moral imperative* that we have it, then is when we join the fashionable madmen, and then is when the thin whine of hysteria is heard in the land, and then is when we are in bad trouble. And I suspect we are already there.

1965

On Going Home

I AM HOME for my daughter's first birthday.
By "home" I do not mean the house in Los
Angeles where my husband and I and the
baby live, but the place where my family is,
in the Central Valley of California. It is a vital although troublesome distinction. My
husband likes my family but is uneasy in
their house, because once there I fall into
their ways, which are difficult, oblique, de-
liberately inarticulate, not my husband's
ways. We live in dusty houses ("D-U-S-T,"
he once wrote with his finger on surfaces all
over the house, but no one noticed it) filled
with mementos quite without value to him
(what could the Canton dessert plates mean
to him? how could he have known about the
assay scales, why should he care if he did
know?), and we appear to talk exclusively
about people we know who have been committed to mental hospitals, about people we
know who have been booked on drunk-

driving charges, and about property, particularly about property, land, price per acre
and C-2 zoning and assessments and freeway access. My brother does not understand
my husband's inability to perceive the advantage in the rather common real-estate
transaction known as "sale-leaseback," and
my husband in turn does not understand
why so many of the people he hears about
in my father's house have recently been
committed to mental hospitals or booked
on drunk-driving charges. Nor does he understand that when we talk about sale-
leasebacks and right-of-way condemnations
we are talking in code about the things we
like best, the yellow fields and the cottonwoods and the rivers rising and falling and
the mountain roads closing when the heavy
snow comes in. We miss each other's points,
have another drink and regard the fire. My
brother refers to my husband, in his presence, as "Joan's husband." Marriage is the
classic betrayal.

Or perhaps it is not any more. Sometimes I think that those of us who are
now in our thirties were born into the last

generation to carry the burden of "home," to find in family life the source of all tension and drama. I had by all objective accounts a "normal" and a "happy" family situation, and yet I was almost thirty years old before I could talk to my family on the telephone without crying after I had hung up. We did not fight. Nothing was wrong. And yet some nameless anxiety colored the emotional charges between me and the place that I came from. The question of whether or not you could go home again was a very real part of the sentimental and largely literary baggage with which we left home in the fifties; I suspect that it is irrelevant to the children born of the fragmentation after World War II. A few weeks ago in a San Francisco bar I saw a pretty young girl on crystal take off her clothes and dance for the cash prize in an "amateur-topless" contest. There was no particular sense of moment about this, none of the effect of romantic degradation, of "dark journey," for which my generation strived so assiduously. What sense could that girl possibly make of, say, *Long Day's Journey into Night?* Who is beside the point?

That I am trapped in this particular irrelevancy is never more apparent to me than when I am home. Paralyzed by the neurotic lassitude engendered by meeting one's past at every turn, around every corner, inside every cupboard, I go aimlessly from room to room. I decide to meet it head-on and clean out a drawer, and I spread the contents on the bed. A bathing suit I wore the summer I was seventeen. A letter of rejection from *The Nation*, an aerial photograph of the site for a shopping center my father did not build in 1954. Three teacups hand-painted with cabbage roses and signed "E.M.," my grandmother's initials. There is no final solution for letters of rejection from *The Nation* and teacups hand-painted in 1900. Nor is there any answer to snapshots of one's grandfather as a young man on skis, surveying around Donner Pass in the year 1910. I smooth out the snapshot and look into his face, and do and do not see my own. I close the drawer, and have another cup of coffee with my mother. We get along very well, veterans of a guerrilla war we never understood.

Days pass. I see no one. I come to dread my husband's evening call, not only because he is full of news of what by now seems to me our remote life in Los Angeles, people he has seen, letters which require attention, but because he asks what I have been doing, suggests uneasily that I get out, drive to San Francisco or Berkeley. Instead I drive across the river to a family graveyard. It has been vandalized since my last visit and the monuments are broken, overturned in the dry grass. Because I once saw a rattlesnake in the grass I stay in the car and listen to a country-and-Western station. Later I drive with my father to a ranch he has in the foothills. The man who runs his cattle on it asks us to the roundup, a week from Sunday, and although I know that I will be in Los Angeles I say, in the oblique way my family talks, that I will come. Once home I mention the broken monuments in the graveyard. My mother shrugs.

I go to visit my great-aunts. A few of them think now that I am my cousin, or their daughter who died young. We recall an anecdote about a relative last seen in

1948, and they ask if I still like living in New York City. I have lived in Los Angeles for three years, but I say that I do. The baby is offered a horehound drop, and I am slipped a dollar bill "to buy a treat." Questions trail off, answers are abandoned, the baby plays with the dust motes in a shaft of afternoon sun.

It is time for the baby's birthday party: a white cake, strawberry-marshmallow ice cream, a bottle of champagne saved from another party. In the evening, after she has gone to sleep, I kneel beside the crib and touch her face, where it is pressed against the slats, with mine. She is an open and trusting child, unprepared for and unaccustomed to the ambushes of family life, and perhaps it is just as well that I can offer her little of that life. I would like to give her more. I would like to promise her that she will grow up with a sense of her cousins and of rivers and of her great-grandmother's teacups, would like to pledge her a picnic on a river with fried chicken and her hair uncombed, would like to give her *home* for her birthday, but we live differently now and I can promise her nothing like that. I give her a xylophone and a sundress from Madeira, and promise to tell her a funny story.

1967

III
SEVEN PLACES
OF THE MIND

Notes from a Native Daughter

IT IS VERY EASY to sit at the bar in, say, La Scala in Beverly Hills, or Ernie's in San Francisco, and to share in the pervasive delusion that California is only five hours from New York by air. The truth is that La Scala and Ernie's are only five hours from New York by air. California is somewhere else.

Many people in the East (or "back East," as they say in California, although not in La Scala or Ernie's) do not believe this. They have been to Los Angeles or to San Francisco, have driven through a giant redwood and have seen the Pacific glazed by the afternoon sun off Big Sur, and they naturally tend to believe that they have in fact been to California. They have not been, and they probably never will be, for it is a longer and in many ways a more difficult trip than they might want to undertake, one of those trips on which the destination flickers chimerically on the horizon, ever receding, ever diminishing. I happen to know about that trip because I come from California, come from a family, or a congeries of families, that has always been in the Sacramento Valley.

You might protest that no family has been in the Sacramento Valley for anything approaching "always." But it is characteristic of Californians to speak grandly of the past as if it had simultaneously begun, *tabula rasa,* and reached a happy ending on the day the wagons started west. *Eureka*—"I Have Found It"—as the state motto has it. Such a view of history casts a certain melancholia over those who participate in it; my own childhood was suffused with the conviction that we had long outlived our finest hour. In fact that is what I want to tell you about: what it is like to come from a place like Sacramento. If I could make you understand that, I could make you understand California and perhaps something else besides, for Sacramento *is* California, and California is a place in which a boom mentality and a sense of Chekhovian loss meet in uneasy suspension; in which the mind is troubled by some buried but ineradicable suspicion that things had better work here, because here, beneath that immense bleached sky, is where we run out of continent.

In 1847 Sacramento was no more than an adobe enclosure, Sutter's Fort, standing alone on the prairie; cut off from San Francisco and the sea by the Coast Range and from the rest of the continent by the Sierra Nevada, the Sacramento Valley was then a true sea of grass, grass so high a man riding into it could tie it across his saddle. A year later gold was discovered in the Sierra foothills, and abruptly Sacramento was a town, a town any moviegoer could map tonight in his dreams—a dusty collage of assay offices and wagonmakers and saloons. Call that Phase Two. Then the settlers came—the farmers, the people who for two hundred years had been moving west on the frontier, the peculiar flawed strain who had cleared Virginia, Kentucky, Missouri; they made Sacramento a farm town. Because the land was rich, Sacramento became eventually a rich farm town, which meant houses in town, Cadillac dealers, a country club. In that gentle sleep Sacramento dreamed until perhaps 1950, when something happened. What happened was that Sacramento woke to the fact that the outside world was moving in, fast and hard. At the moment of its waking Sacramento lost, for better or for worse, its character, and that is part of what I want to tell you about.

But the change is not what I remember first. First I remember running a boxer dog of my brother's over the same flat fields that our great-great-grandfather had found virgin and had planted; I remember swimming (albeit nervously, for I was a nervous child, afraid of sinkholes and afraid of snakes, and perhaps that was the beginning of my error) the same rivers we had swum for a century: the Sacramento, so rich with silt that we could barely see our hands a few inches beneath the surface; the American, running clean and fast with melted Sierra snow until July, when it would slow down, and rattlesnakes would sun themselves on its newly exposed rocks. The Sacramento, the American, sometimes the Cosumnes, occasionally the Feather. Incautious children died every day in those rivers; we read about it in the paper, how they had miscalculated a current or stepped into a hole down where the American runs into the Sacramento, how the Berry Brothers had been called in from Yolo County to drag the river but how the bodies remained unrecovered. "They were from away," my grandmother would extrapolate from the newspaper stories. "Their parents had no *business* letting them in the river. They were visitors from Omaha." It was not a bad lesson, although a less than reliable one; children we knew died in the rivers too.

When summer ended—when the State Fair closed and the heat broke, when the last green hop vines had been torn down along the H Street road and the tule fog began rising off the low ground at night—we would go back to memorizing the Products of Our Latin American Neighbors and to visiting the great-aunts on Sunday, dozens of great-aunts, year after year of Sundays. When I think now of those winters I think of yellow elm leaves wadded in the gutters outside the Trinity Episcopal Pro-Cathedral on M Street. There are actually people in Sacramento now who call M Street Capitol Avenue, and Trinity has one of those featureless new buildings, but perhaps children still learn the same things there on Sunday mornings:

> Q. In what way does the Holy Land resemble the Sacramento Valley?
> A. In the type and diversity of its agricultural products.

And I think of the rivers rising, of listening to the radio to hear at what height they would crest and wondering if and when and where the levees would go. We did not have as many dams in those years. The bypasses would be full, and men would sandbag all night. Sometimes a levee would go in the night, somewhere upriver; in the morning the rumor would spread that the Army Engineers had dynamited it to relieve the pressure on the city.

After the rains came spring, for ten days
or so; the drenched fields would dissolve
into a brilliant ephemeral green (it would be
yellow and dry as fire in two or three weeks)
and the real-estate business would pick up.
It was the time of year when people's grandmothers went to Carmel; it was the time of
year when girls who could not even get into
Stephens or Arizona or Oregon, let alone
Stanford or Berkeley, would be sent to Honolulu, on the *Lurline*. I have no recollection
of anyone going to New York, with the ex-
ception of a cousin who visited there (I cannot imagine why) and reported that the
shoe salesmen at Lord & Taylor were "intol-
erably rude." What happened in New York
and Washington and abroad seemed to im-
pinge not at all upon the Sacramento mind.
I remember being taken to call upon a very
old woman, a rancher's widow, who was
reminiscing (the favored conversational
mode in Sacramento) about the son of some
contemporaries of hers. "That Johnston boy
never did amount to much," she said. Desultorily, my mother protested: Alva Johnston, she said, had won the Pulitzer Prize,

when he was working for *The New York Times*. Our hostess looked at us impassively. "He never amounted to anything in Sacramento," she said.

Hers was the true Sacramento voice, and, although I did not realize it then, one not long to be heard, for the war was over and the boom was on and the voice of the aerospace engineer would be heard in the land. VETS NO DOWN! EXECUTIVE LIVING ON LOW FHA!

Later, when I was living in New York, I would make the trip back to Sacramento four and five times a year (the more comfortable the flight, the more obscurely miserable I would be, for it weighs heavily upon my kind that we could perhaps not make it by wagon), trying to prove that I had not meant to leave at all, because in at least one respect California—the California we are talking about—resembles Eden: it is assumed that those who absent themselves from its blessings have been banished, exiled by some perversity of heart. Did not the Donner-Reed Party, after all, eat its own dead to reach Sacramento?

I have said that the trip back is difficult, and it is—difficult in a way that magnifies the ordinary ambiguities of sentimental journeys. Going back to California is not like going back to Vermont, or Chicago; Vermont and Chicago are relative constants, against which one measures one's own change. All that is constant about the California of my childhood is the rate at which it disappears. An instance: on Saint Patrick's Day of 1948 I was taken to see the legislature "in action," a dismal experience; a handful of florid assemblymen, wearing green hats, were reading Pat-and-Mike jokes into the record. I still think of the legislators that way—wearing green hats, or sitting around on the veranda of the Senator Hotel fanning themselves and being entertained by Artie Samish's emissaries. (Samish was the lobbyist who said, "Earl Warren may be the governor of the state, but I'm the governor of the legislature.") In fact there is no longer a veranda at the

Senator Hotel—it was turned into an airline ticket office, if you want to embroider the point—and in any case the legislature has largely deserted the Senator for the flashy motels north of town, where the tiki torches flame and the steam rises off the heated swimming pools in the cold Valley night.

It is hard to *find* California now, unsettling to wonder how much of it was merely imagined or improvised; melancholy to realize how much of anyone's memory is no true memory at all but only the traces of someone else's memory, stories handed down on the family network. I have an indelibly vivid "memory," for example, of how Prohibition affected the hop growers around Sacramento: the sister of a grower my family knew brought home a mink coat from San Francisco, and was told to take it back, and sat on the floor of the parlor cradling that coat and crying. Although I was not born until a year after Repeal, that scene is more "real" to me than many I have played myself.

I remember one trip home, when I sat alone on a night jet from New York and read over and over some lines from a W. S. Merwin poem I had come across in a magazine, a poem about a man who had been a long time in another country and knew that he must go home:

> . . . *But it should be*
> *Soon. Already I defend hotly*
> *Certain of our indefensible faults,*
> *Resent being reminded; already in my*
>   *mind*
> *Our language becomes freighted with a*
>   *richness*
> *No common tongue could offer, while*
>   *the mountains*
> *Are like nowhere on earth, and the*
>   *wide rivers.*

You see the point. I want to tell you the truth, and already I have told you about the wide rivers.

It should be clear by now that the truth about the place is elusive, and must be tracked with caution. You might go to Sacramento tomorrow and someone (although no one I know) might take you out to Aerojet-General, which has, in the Sacramento phrase, "something to do with rockets." Fifteen thousand people work for Aerojet, almost all of them imported; a Sacramento lawyer's wife told me, as evidence of how Sacramento was opening up, that she believed she had met one of them, at an open house two Decembers ago. ("Couldn't have been nicer, actually," she added enthusiastically. "I think he and his wife bought the house next *door* to Mary and Al, something like that, which of course was how *they* met him.") So you might go to Aerojet and stand in the big vendors' lobby where a couple of thousand components salesmen try every week to sell their wares and you might look up at the electrical wallboard that lists Aerojet personnel, their projects and their location at any given time, and you might wonder if I have been in Sacramento lately. MINUTEMAN, POLARIS, TITAN, the lights flash, and all the coffee tables are littered with airline schedules, very now, very much in touch.

But I could take you a few miles from there into towns where the banks still bear names like The Bank of Alex Brown, into towns where the one hotel still has an octagonal-tile floor in the dining room and dusty potted palms and big ceiling fans; into towns where everything—the seed business, the Harvester franchise, the hotel, the department store and the main street—carries a single name, the name of the man who built the town. A few Sundays ago I was in a town like that, a town smaller than that, really, no hotel, no Harvester franchise, the bank burned out, a river town. It was the golden anniversary of some of my relatives and it was 110° and the guests of honor sat on straight-backed chairs in front of a sheaf of gladioluses in the Rebekah Hall. I mentioned visiting Aerojet-General to a cousin I saw there, who listened to me with interested disbelief. Which is the true California? That is what we all wonder.

Let us try out a few irrefutable statements, on subjects not open to interpretation. Although Sacramento is in many ways the least typical of the Valley towns, it *is* a Valley town, and must be viewed in that context. When you say "the Valley" in Los Angeles, most people assume that you mean the San Fernando Valley (some people in fact assume that you mean Warner Brothers), but make no mistake: we are talking not about the valley of the sound stages and the ranchettes but about the real Valley, the Central Valley, the fifty thousand square miles drained by the Sacramento and the San Joaquin Rivers and further irrigated by a complex network of sloughs, cutoffs, ditches, and the Delta-Mendota and Friant-Kern Canals.

A hundred miles north of Los Angeles, at the moment when you drop from the Tehachapi Mountains into the outskirts of Bakersfield, you leave Southern California and enter the Valley. "You look up the highway and it is straight for miles, coming at you, with the black line down the center coming at you and at you . . . and the heat dazzles up from the white slab so that only the black line is clear, coming at you with the whine of the tires, and if you don't quit staring at that line and don't take a few deep breaths and slap yourself hard on the back of the neck you'll hypnotize yourself."

Robert Penn Warren wrote that about another road, but he might have been writing about the Valley road, U.S. 99, three hundred miles from Bakersfield to Sacramento, a highway so straight that when one flies on the most direct pattern from Los Angeles to Sacramento one never loses sight of U.S. 99. The landscape it runs through never, to the untrained eye, varies. The Valley eye can discern the point where miles of cotton seedlings fade into miles of tomato seedlings, or where the great corporation ranches—Kern County Land, what is left of DiGiorgio—give way to private operations (somewhere on the horizon, if the place is private, one sees a house and a stand of scrub oaks), but such distinctions are in the long view irrelevant. All day long, all that moves is the sun, and the big Rainbird sprinklers.

Every so often along 99 between Bakersfield and Sacramento there is a town: Delano, Tulare, Fresno, Madera, Merced, Modesto, Stockton. Some of these towns are pretty big now, but they are all the same at heart, one- and two- and three-story buildings artlessly arranged, so that what appears to be the good dress shop stands beside a W. T. Grant store, so that the big Bank of America faces a Mexican movie house. *Dos Peliculas, Bingo Bingo Bingo.* Beyond the downtown (pronounced *downtown*, with the Okie accent that now pervades Valley speech patterns) lie blocks of old frame houses—paint peeling, sidewalks cracking, their occasional leaded amber windows overlooking a Foster's Freeze or a five-minute car wash or a State Farm Insurance office; beyond those spread the shopping centers and the miles of tract houses, pastel with redwood siding, the unmistakable signs of cheap building already blossoming on those houses which have survived the first rain. To a stranger driving 99 in an air-conditioned car (he would be on business, I suppose, any stranger driving 99, for 99 would never get a tourist to Big Sur or San Simeon, never get him to the California he came to see), these towns must seem so flat, so impoverished, as to drain the imagination. They hint at evenings spent hanging around gas stations, and suicide pacts sealed in drive-ins.

But remember:

Q. In what way does the Holy Land resemble the Sacramento Valley?
A. In the type and diversity of its agricultural products.

U.S. 99 in fact passes through the richest and most intensely cultivated agricultural region in the world, a giant outdoor hothouse with a billion-dollar crop. It is when you remember the Valley's wealth that the monochromatic flatness of its towns takes on a curious meaning, suggests a habit of mind some would consider perverse. There is something in the Valley mind that reflects a real indifference to the stranger in his air-conditioned car, a failure to perceive even his presence, let alone his thoughts or wants. An implacable insularity is the seal of these towns. I once met a woman in Dallas, a most charming and attractive woman accustomed to the hospitality and social hypersensitivity of Texas, who told me that during the four war years her husband had been stationed in Modesto, she had never once been invited inside anyone's house. No one in Sacramento would find this story remarkable ("She probably had no *relatives* there," said someone to whom I told it), for the Valley towns understand one another, share a peculiar spirit. They think alike and they look alike. *I* can tell Modesto from Merced, but I have visited there, gone to dances there; besides, there is over the main street of Modesto an arched sign which reads:

WATER—WEALTH
CONTENTMENT—HEALTH

There is no such sign in Merced.

I said that Sacramento was the least typical of the Valley towns, and it is—but only because it is bigger and more diverse, only because it has had the rivers and the legislature; its true character remains the Valley character, its virtues the Valley virtues, its sadness the Valley sadness. It is just as hot in the summertime, so hot that the air shimmers and the grass bleaches white and the blinds stay drawn all day, so hot that August comes on not like a month but like an affliction; it is just as flat, so flat that a ranch of my family's with a slight rise on it, perhaps a foot, was known for the hundred-some years which preceded this year as "the hill ranch." (It is known this year as a sub-division in the making, but that is another part of the story.) Above all, in spite of its infusions from outside, Sacramento retains the Valley insularity.

To sense that insularity a visitor need do no more than pick up a copy of either of the two newspapers, the morning *Union* or the afternoon *Bee*. The *Union* happens to be Republican and impoverished and the *Bee* Democratic and powerful ("THE VALLEY OF THE BEES!" as the McClatchys, who own the Fresno, Modesto, and Sacramento *Bees*, used to headline their advertisements in the trade press. "ISOLATED FROM ALL OTHER MEDIA INFLUENCE!"), but they read a good deal alike, and the tone of their chief editorial concerns is strange and wonderful and instructive. The *Union*, in a county heavily and reliably Democratic, frets mainly about the possibility of a local takeover by the John Birch Society; the *Bee*, faithful to the letter of its founder's will, carries on overwrought crusades against phantoms it still calls "the power trusts." Shades of Hiram Johnson, whom the *Bee* helped elect governor in 1910. Shades of Robert La Follette, to whom the *Bee* delivered the Valley in 1924. There is something about the Sacramento papers that does not quite connect with the way Sacramento lives now, something pronouncedly beside the point. The aerospace engineers, one learns, read the San Francisco *Chronicle*.

The Sacramento papers, however, simply mirror the Sacramento peculiarity, the Valley fate, which is to be paralyzed by a past no longer relevant. Sacramento is a town which grew up on farming and discovered to its shock that land has more profitable uses. (The chamber of commerce will give you crop figures, but pay them no mind— what matters is the feeling, the knowledge that where the green hops once grew is now Larchmont Riviera, that what used to be the Whitney ranch is now Sunset City, thirty-three thousand houses and a country-club complex.) It is a town in which defense industry and its absentee owners are suddenly the most important facts; a town which has never had more people or more money, but has lost its *raison d'être*. It is a town many of whose most solid citizens sense about themselves a kind of functional obsolescence. The old families still see only one another, but they do not see even one another as much as they once did; they are closing ranks, preparing for the long night, selling their rights-of-way and living on the proceeds. Their children still marry one another, still play bridge and go into the real-estate business together. (There is no other business in Sacramento, no reality other than land—even I, when I was living and working in New York, felt impelled to take a University of California correspondence course in Urban Land Economics.) But late at night when the ice has melted there is always somebody now, some Julian English, whose heart is not quite in it. For out there on the outskirts of town are marshaled the legions of aerospace engineers, who talk their peculiar condescending language and tend their dichondra and plan to stay in the promised land; who are raising a new generation of native Sacramentans and who do not care, really do not care, that they are not asked to join the Sutter Club. It makes one wonder, late at night when the ice is gone; introduces some air into the womb, suggests that the Sutter Club is perhaps not, after all, the Pacific Union or the Bohemian; that Sacramento is not *the city*. In just such self-doubts do small towns lose their character.

I want to tell you a Sacramento story. A few miles out of town is a place, six or seven thousand acres, which belonged in the beginning to a rancher with one daughter. That daughter went abroad and married a title, and when she brought the title home to live on the ranch, her father built them a vast house—music rooms, conservatories, a ballroom. They needed a ballroom because they entertained: people from abroad, people from San Francisco, house parties that lasted weeks and involved special trains. They are long dead, of course, but their only son, aging and unmarried, still lives on the place. He does not live in the house, for the house is no longer there. Over the years it burned, room by room, wing by wing. Only the chimneys of the great house are still standing, and its heir lives in their shadow, lives by himself on the charred site, in a house trailer.

That is a story my generation knows; I doubt that the next will know it, the children of the aerospace engineers. Who would tell it to them? Their grandmothers live in Scarsdale, and they have never met a great-aunt. "Old" Sacramento to them will be something colorful, something they read about in *Sunset*. They will probably think that the Redevelopment has always been there, that the Embarcadero, down along the river, with its amusing places to shop and its picturesque fire houses turned into bars, has about it the true flavor of the way it was. There will be no reason for them to know that in homelier days it was called Front Street (the town was not, after all, settled by the Spanish) and was a place of derelicts and missions and itinerant pickers in town for a Saturday-night drunk: VICTORIOUS LIFE MISSION, JESUS SAVES, BEDS 25¢ A NIGHT, CROP INFORMATION HERE. They will have lost the real past and gained a manufactured one, and there will be no way for them to know, no way at all, why a house trailer should stand alone on seven thousand acres outside town.

But perhaps it is presumptuous of me to assume that they will be missing something.

Perhaps in retrospect this has been a story not about Sacramento at all, but about the things we lose and the promises we break as we grow older; perhaps I have been playing out unawares the Margaret in the poem:

> *Margaret, are you grieving*
> *Over Goldengrove unleaving? . . .*
> *It is the blight man was born for,*
> *It is Margaret you mourn for.*

1965

Letter from Paradise,
21° 19' N., 157° 52' W.

BECAUSE I HAD BEEN TIRED too long and quarrelsome too much and too often frightened of migraine and failure and the days getting shorter, I was sent, a recalcitrant thirty-one-year-old child, to Hawaii, where winter does not come and no one fails and the median age is twenty-three. There I could become a new woman, there with the life-insurance salesmen on million-dollar-a-year incentive trips, there with the Shriners and the San Francisco divorcées and the splurging secretaries and the girls in the string bikinis and the boys in search of the perfect wave, children who understood the insouciant economy of buying a Honda or a surfboard for one dollar down and $2.50 a week and then abandoning it, children who have never been told, as I was told, that golden lads and girls all must as chimney sweepers come to dust. I was to lie beneath the same sun that had kept Doris Duke and

Henry Kaiser forever hopeful. I was to play at sipping frozen daiquiris and wear flowers in my hair as if ten years had never happened. I was to see for myself that just beyond the end of the line lay not Despond but Diamond Head.

I went, a wary visitor. I do not believe that the stories told by lovely hula hands merit extensive study. I have never heard a Hawaiian word, including and perhaps most particularly *aloha*, which accurately expressed anything I had to say. I have neither enough capacity for surprise nor enough heart for twice-told tales to make you listen again to tedious vignettes about Midwesterners in souvenir shirts and touring widows in muumuus and simulated pearls, about the Kodak Hula Show or the Sunday Night Luau or the Schoolteacher and the Beach Boy. And so, now that it is on the line between us that I lack all temperament for paradise, real or facsimile, I am going to find it difficult to tell you precisely how and why Hawaii moves me, touches me, saddens and troubles and engages my imagination, what it is in the air that will

linger long after I have forgotten the smell
of pikake and pineapple and the way the
palms sound in the trade winds.

Perhaps because I grew up in California,
Hawaii figured large in my fantasies. I sat as
a child on California beaches and imagined
that I saw Hawaii, a certain shimmer in the
sunset, a barely perceptible irregularity
glimpsed intermittently through squinted
eyes. The curious void in this fantasy was
that I had not the slightest idea what Hawaii would look like if I did see it, for in my
child's mind there were three distant Ha-
waiis, and I could perceive no connections
among the three.

There was, to begin with, the Hawaii
first shown to me in an atlas on December 7,
1941, the pastel pinpoints that meant war
and my father going away and makeshift
Christmases in rented rooms near Air Corps
bases and nothing the same ever again.
Later, when the war was over, there was
another Hawaii, a big rock candy mountain in the Pacific which presented itself to
me in newspaper photographs of well-fed
Lincoln-Mercury dealers relaxing beside

an outrigger at the Royal Hawaiian Hotel or disembarking *en famille* from the *Lurline*, a Hawaii where older cousins might spend winter vacations learning to surfboard (for that is what it was called in those simpler days, surfboarding, and it was peculiar to Hawaii) and where godmothers might repair to rest and to learn all the lyrics to "My Little Grass Shack in Kealakekua Hawaii." I do not remember how many nights I lay awake in bed and listened to someone downstairs singing "My Little Grass Shack in Kealakekua Hawaii," but I do remember that I made no connection between that Hawaii and the Hawaii of December 7, 1941.

And then, always, there was a third Hawaii, a place which seemed to have to do neither with war nor with vacationing godmothers but only with the past, and with loss. The last member of my direct family ever to live in Hawaii was a great-great-grandfather who taught there as a young missionary in 1842, and I was given to understand that life in the Islands, as we called Hawaii on the West Coast, had been declining steadily since. My aunt married into a family which had lived for generations in the Islands, but they did not even visit there any more; "Not since Mr. *Kaiser*," they would say, as if the construction of the Hawaiian Village Hotel on a few acres of reclaimed tidal flat near Fort De Russy had in one swing of the builder's crane wiped out their childhoods and their parents' childhoods, blighted forever some subtropical cherry orchard where every night in the soft blur of memory the table was set for forty-eight in case someone dropped by; as if Henry Kaiser had personally condemned them to live out their lives in California exile among only their token mementos, the calabashes and the carved palace chairs and the flat silver for forty-eight and the diamond that had been Queen Liliuokalani's and the heavy linens embroidered on all the long golden afternoons that were no more.

Of course as I grew older I recognized that the name "Henry Kaiser" carried more symbolic than literal freight, but even then I missed the point, imagined that it was merely the proliferation of hotels and hundred-dollar thrift flights that had disturbed the old order, managed to dismiss the Hawaii of my first memory, the Hawaii which meant war, as an accident of history, a freak relevant neither to the gentle idyll that must have been the past nor to the frenetic paean to middle-income leisure that must be the present. In so doing I misapprehended Hawaii completely, for if there is a single aura which pervades Honolulu, one mood which lends the lights a feverish luster and the pink catamarans a heartbreaking absurdity and which engages the imagination as mere paradise never could, that mood is, inescapably, one of war.

It begins, of course, in what we remember.

Hawaii is our Gibraltar, and almost our Channel Coast. Planes, their eyes sharpened by the year-round clearness of blue Pacific days, can keep easy watch over an immense sea-circle, of which Hawaii is the centre. With Hawaii on guard, a surprise attack on us from Asia, the experts believe, would be quite impossible. So long as the great Pearl Harbor Naval Base, just down the road from Honolulu, is ours, American warships and submarines can run their un-Pacific errands with a maximum of ease. Pearl Harbor is one of the greatest, if not the very greatest, maritime fortresses in the world. Pearl Harbor has immense reserves of fuel and food, and huge and clanging hospitals for the healing of any wounds which steel can suffer. It is the one sure sanctuary in the whole of the vast Pacific both for ships and men.

John W. Vandercook; in
Vogue, January 1, 1941

Every afternoon now, twenty-five years after the fact, the bright pink tour boats leave Kewalo Basin for Pearl Harbor. It has a kind of sleazy festivity at first, the prospect of an outing on a fine day, the passengers comparing complaints about their tour directors and their accommodations and the food at Canlis' Charcoal Broiler, the boys diving for coins around the boats; "Hey Mister Big," they scream. "How's about a coin." Sometimes a woman will throw a bill, and then be outraged when the insolent brown bodies pluck it from the air and jeer at her expectations. As the boat leaves the basin the boys swim back, their cheeks stuffed with money, and the children pout that they would rather be at the beach, and the women in their new Liberty House shifts and leftover leis sip papaya juice and study a booklet billed as *An Ideal Gift— Picture Story of December 7.*

It is, after all, a familiar story that we have come to hear—familiar even to the children, for of course they have seen John Wayne and John Garfield at Pearl Harbor, have spent countless rainy afternoons watching Kirk Douglas and Spencer Tracy and Van Johnson wonder out loud why Hickam does not answer this morning— and no one listens very closely to the guide.

Sugar cane now blows where the *Nevada* went aground. An idle figure practices putting on Ford Island. The concessionaire breaks out more papaya juice. It is hard to remember what we came to remember.

And then something happens. I took that bright pink boat to Pearl Harbor on two afternoons, but I still do not know what I went to find out, which is how other people respond a quarter of a century later. I do not know because there is a point at which I began to cry, and to notice no one else. I began to cry at the place where the *Utah* lies in fifty feet of water, water neither turquoise nor bright blue here but the gray of harbor waters everywhere, and I did not stop until after the pink boat had left the *Arizona*, or what is visible of the *Arizona*: the rusted after-gun turret breaking the gray water, the flag at full mast because the Navy considers the *Arizona* still in commission, a full crew aboard, 1,102 men from forty-nine states. All I know about how other people respond is what I am told: that everyone is quiet at the *Arizona*.

A few days ago someone just four years younger than I am told me that he did not see why a sunken ship should affect me so, that John Kennedy's assassination, not Pearl Harbor, was the single most indelible event of what he kept calling "our generation." I could tell him only that we belonged to different generations, and I did not tell him what I want to tell you, about a place in Honolulu that is quieter still than the *Arizona*: the National Memorial Cemetery of the Pacific. They all seem to be twenty years old, the boys buried up there in the crater of an extinct volcano named Punchbowl, twenty and nineteen and eighteen and sometimes not that old. "SAMUEL FOSTER HARMON," one stone reads. "PENNSYLVANIA. PVT 27 REPL DRAFT 5 MARINE DIV. WORLD WAR II. APRIL 10 1928—MARCH 25 1945." Samuel Foster Harmon died, at Iwo Jima, fifteen days short of his seventeenth birthday. Some of them died on December 7 and some of them died after the

Enola Gay had already bombed Hiroshima and some of them died on the dates of the landings at Okinawa and Iwo Jima and Guadalcanal and one whole long row of them, I am told, died on the beach of an island we no longer remember. There are 19,000 graves in the vast sunken crater above Honolulu.

I would go up there quite a bit. If I walked to the rim of the crater I could see the city, look down over Waikiki and the harbor and the jammed arterials, but up there it was quiet, and high enough into the rain forest so that a soft mist falls most of the day. One afternoon a couple came and left three plumeria leis on the grave of a California boy who had been killed, at nineteen, in 1945. The leis were already wilting by the time the woman finally placed them on the grave, because for a long time she only stood there and twisted them in her hands. On the whole I am able to take a very long view of death, but I think a great deal about what there is to remember, twenty-one years later, of a boy who died at nineteen. I saw no one else there but the men who cut the grass and the men who dig new graves, for they are bringing in bodies now from Vietnam. The graves filled last week and the week before that and even last month do not yet have stones, only plastic identification cards, streaked by the mist and splattered with mud. The earth is raw and trampled in that part of the crater, but the grass grows fast, up there in the rain cloud.

It is not very far from the crater down to Hotel Street, which is to Honolulu what Market Street is to San Francisco, the bright night street in a port city. The carrier *Coral Sea* was in Honolulu that week, and 165 men in from Vietnam on rest-and-recuperation leave, and 3,500 Marines on their way to Okinawa and then to Vietnam (they were part of the reactivated 5th Marine Division, and it was the 5th, if you will remember, to which the sixteen-year-old Samuel Foster Harmon belonged), and besides that there was the regular complement of personnel for Pearl and Hickam and Camp H. M. Smith and Fort Shafter and Fort De Russy and Bellows A.F.B. and the Kaneohe Marine Air Station and Schofield

Barracks, and sooner or later they all got downtown to Hotel Street. They always have. The Navy cleaned out the red-light houses at the end of World War II, but the Hotel Streets of this world do not change perceptibly from war to war. The girls with hibiscus in their hair stroll idly in front of the penny arcades and the Japanese pool halls and the massage studios. "GIRLS WANTED FOR MASSAGE WORK," the signs say. "WHAT A REFRESHING NEW TINGLE." The fortunetellers sit and file their nails behind flowered paper curtains. The boys from the cast of the Boys Will Be Girls Revue stand out on the sidewalk in lamé evening dresses, smoking cigarettes and looking the sailors over.

And the sailors get drunk. They all seem to be twenty years old on Hotel Street, too, twenty and nineteen and eighteen and drunk because they are no longer in Des Moines and not yet in Danang. They look in at the taxi-dance places and they look in at the strip places with the pictures of Lili St. Cyr and Tempest Storm outside (Lili St. Cyr was in California and Tempest Storm in Baltimore, but never mind, they all look alike on Saturday night in Honolulu) and they fish in their pockets for quarters to see the Art Movie in the back of the place that sells *Sunshine* and *Nude* and all the paperbacks with chained girls on the cover. They have snapshots laminated. They record their own voices (*Hi, Sweetheart, I'm in Honolulu tonight*) and they talk to the girls with hibiscus in their hair.

But mostly they just get a little drunker, and jostle around on the sidewalk avoiding the Hawaii Armed Forces Patrol and daring one another to get tattooed. In a show of bravado they rip off their shirts a half block before they reach Lou Normand's Tattoo Parlor and then they sit with glazed impassivity while the needle brands them with a heart or an anchor or, if they are particularly flush or particularly drunk, a replica of Christ on the cross with the stigmata in red. Their friends cluster outside the glass cubicle watching the skin redden and all the while, from a country-and-western bar on the corner, "King of the Road" reverberates down Hotel Street. The songs change and the boys come and go but Lou Normand has been Thirty Years in the Same Location.

Perhaps it seems not surprising that there should be a mood of war at the scenes of famous defeats and at the graves of seventeen-year-olds and downtown in a port city. But the mood is not only there. War is in the very fabric of Hawaii's life, ineradicably fixed in both its emotions and its economy, dominating not only its memory but its vision of the future. There is a point at which every Honolulu conversation refers back to war. People sit in their gardens up on Makiki Heights among their copa de oro and their star jasmine and they look down toward Pearl Harbor and get another drink and tell you about the morning it happened. Webley Edwards was on the radio, they remember that, and what he said that morning again and again was "This is an air raid, take cover, *this is the real McCoy.*" That is not a remarkable thing to say, but it is a remarkable thing to have in one's memory. And they remember how people drove up into the hills and parked to watch the fires, just as they do now when a tsunami wave is due. They remember emergency wards in school auditoriums and how the older children were dispatched to guard reservoirs with unloaded guns. They laugh about trying to drive over the Pali in the fog after the 9 p.m. blackout, and about how their wives took thick books and large handkerchiefs down to the Y.W.C.A. and used them to show girls from the outer islands how to make a hospital bed, and they remember how it was when there were only three hotels on all two miles of Waikiki, the Royal for the Navy, the Halekulani for the press, and the Moana. In fact they contrive to leave an indistinct impression that it was in 1945, or perhaps '46, that they last got down to Waikiki. "I suppose the Royal hasn't changed," one Honolulan who lives within eight minutes of the Royal remarked to me. "The Halekulani," another said, as if it had just flickered into memory and she was uncertain it still existed.

"*That* used to be kind of fun for drinks." Everyone was younger then, and in the telling a certain glow suffuses those years.

And then, if they have a stake in selling Hawaii, and there are very few people left in Hawaii who refuse to perceive that they do have a stake in selling it, they explain why Hawaii's future is so bright. In spite of what might be considered a classic false economy, based first upon the military, next upon the tourist, and third upon subsidized sugar, Hawaii's future is bright because Hawaii is the hub of the Pacific, a phrase employed in Honolulu only slightly less frequently than "our wonderful *aloha* spirit." They point out that Hawaii is the hub of the Pacific as far as the travel industry goes, and that Hawaii is also the hub of the Pacific as far as—they pause, and perhaps pick up a glass and study it before continuing. "And, well, frankly, if it goes the other way, what I mean by that is if the *situation* goes the other way, we're in the right spot for that, too." Perhaps nowhere else in the United States is the prospect of war regarded with so much equanimity.

Of course it is easy to suggest reasons, to

say that after all Hawaii has already lived through one war, or to point out that Honolulu is even now in a war zone, steeped in the vocabulary of the military, deeply committed to the business of war. But it runs deeper than that. War is viewed with a curious ambivalence in Hawaii because the largest part of its population interprets war, however unconsciously, as a force for good, an instrument of social progress. And of course it was precisely World War II which cracked the spine of sugar feudalism, opened up a contracting economy and an immobile society, shattered forever the pleasant but formidable colonial world in which a handful of families controlled everything Hawaii did, where it shopped, how it shipped its goods, who could come in and how far they could go and at what point they would be closed out.

We have, most of us, some image of prewar Hawaii. We have heard the phrase "Big Five," and we have a general notion that certain families acquired a great deal of money and power in Hawaii and kept that money and that power for a very long while. The reality of Hawaiian power was at once more obvious and more subtle than one might imagine it to have been. The Big Five companies—C. Brewer, Theo. H. Davies, American Factors, Castle & Cooke, and Alexander & Baldwin—began as "factors" for the sugar planters; in effect they were plantation management. Over the years, the Big Five families and a few others—the Dillinghams, say, who were descended from a stranded sailor who built Hawaii's first railroad—intermarried, sat on one another's boards, got into shipping and insurance and money, and came to comprise a benevolent oligarchy unlike any on the mainland.

For almost half a century this interlocking directorate extended into every area of Hawaiian life, and its power could be exercised immediately and personally. American Factors, for example, owned (and still owns) the major Hawaiian department store, Liberty House. In 1941, Sears, Roebuck, working secretly through intermediaries, bought land for a store in suburban Honolulu. Sears finally opened its store, but not until the Sears president, Robert E.

Wood, had threatened to buy his own ship; there had been some question as to whether Matson Navigation, controlled by Castle & Cooke and Alexander & Baldwin, would ship merchandise for anyone so baldly attempting to compete with a Big Five enterprise.

That was Hawaii. And then World War II came. Island boys went to war, and came home with new ideas. Mainland money came in, against all Island opposition. After World War II, the late Walter Dillingham could come down to a public hearing from his house on Diamond Head and cast at Henry Kaiser the most meaningful epithet of ante-bellum Hawaii—*"visitor"*—and have its significance lost on perhaps half his audience. In spirit if never quite in fact, World War II made everyone a Dillingham, and anyone in Hawaii too slow to perceive this for himself was constantly told it, by politicians and by labor leaders and by mainland observers.

The extent of the change, of course, has often been overstated, for reasons sometimes sentimental and sometimes strategic, but it is true that Hawaii is no more what it once was. There is still only one "Lowell" in Honolulu, and that is Lowell Dillingham, still only one "Ben," and that is his brother—but Ben Dillingham was overwhelmingly defeated in his 1962 campaign for the United States Senate by Daniel Inouye, a Nisei. (In the 1920's, when a congressional committee asked Ben Dillingham's father and Henry Baldwin why so few Japanese voted in Hawaii, they could suggest only that perhaps the Japanese were under instructions from Tokyo not to register.) There is still a strong feeling in old-line Honolulu that the Big Five "caved in" to labor—but Jack Hall, the tough I.L.W.U. leader who was once convicted under the Smith Act for conspiring to teach the overthrow of the United States Government by force and violence, now sits on the board of the Hawaii Visitors' Bureau and commends the ladies of the Outdoor Circle for their efforts in "preserving the loveliness that is Hawaii." And Chinn Ho, who as a schoolboy used to chalk up quotations for a downtown broker, now owns not only a few score million dollars' worth of real estate but also that broker's own house, out on Diamond Head, hard by Ben Dillingham's. "The thing is," the broker's niece told me, "I suppose he wanted it when he was fourteen."

But perhaps there is no clearer way to understand the change than to visit Punahou School, the school the missionaries founded "for their children and their children's children," a statement of purpose interpreted rather literally until quite recently. To leaf through Punahou's old class books is a briefing in Hawaiian oligarchy, for the same names turn up year after year, and the names are the same as those which appear in cut stone or discreet brass letters down around what Honolulu calls The Street, Merchant Street, down on those corners where the Big Five have their offices and most Island business is done. In 1881 an Alexander delivered the commencement address and a Dillingham the commencement poem; at the 1882 graduation a Baldwin spoke on "Chinese Immigration," an Alexander on "Labor Ipse Voluptas," and a Bishop on "Sunshine." And although high-caste

Hawaiians have always coexisted with and in fact intermarried with the white oligarchy, their Punahou classmates usually visualized them, when it came time for class prophecies, "playing in a band."

It is not that Punahou is not still the school of the Island power elite; it is. "There will always be room at Punahou for those children who belong here," Dr. John Fox, headmaster since 1944, assured alumni in a recent bulletin. But where in 1944 there were 1,100 students and they had a median IQ of 108, now there are 3,400 with a median IQ of 125. Where once the enrollment was ten percent Oriental, now it is a fraction under thirty percent. And so it is that outside Punahou's new Cooke Library, where the archives are kept by a great-great-granddaughter of the Reverend Hiram Bingham, there sit, among the plumeria blossoms drifted on the steps, small Chinese boys with their books in Pan American flight bags.

"John Fox is rather controversial, I guess you know," old-family alumni will sometimes say now, but they do not say exactly wherein the controversy lies. Perhaps because Hawaii sells itself so assiduously as the very model of a modern melting pot, the entire area of race relations is conversationally delicate. "I wouldn't exactly say we had discrimination here," one Honolulu woman explained tactfully. "I'd say we had a wonderful, wonderful competitive feeling." Another simply shrugs. "It's just something that's never pressed. The Orientals are—well, discreet's not really the word, but they aren't like the Negroes and the Jews, they don't push in where they're not wanted."

Even among those who are considered Island liberals, the question of race has about it, to anyone who has lived through these hypersensitive past years on the mainland, a curious and rather engaging ingenuousness. "There are very definitely people here who know the Chinese socially," one woman told me. "They have them to their houses. The uncle of a friend of mine, for example, has Chinn Ho to his house all the time." Although this seemed a statement along the lines of "Some of my best friends are Rothschilds," I accepted it in the spirit in which it was offered—just as I did the primitive progressivism of an Island teacher who was explaining, as we walked down a corridor of her school, about the miracles of educational integration the war had wrought. "Look," she said suddenly, grabbing a pretty Chinese girl by the arm and wheeling her around to face me. "You wouldn't have seen this here before the war. Look at those eyes."

And so, in the peculiar and still insular mythology of Hawaii, the dislocations of war became the promises of progress. Whether or not the promises have been fulfilled depends of course upon who is talking, as does whether or not progress is a virtue, but in any case it is war that is pivotal to the Hawaiian imagination, war that fills the mind, war that fills the mind, war that seems to hover over Honolulu like the rain clouds on Tantalus. Not very many people talk about that. They talk about freeways on Oahu and condominiums on Maui and beer cans at the Sacred Falls and how much wiser it is to bypass Honolulu altogether in favor of going directly to Laurance Rockefeller's Mauna Kea, on Hawaii. (In fact the notion that the only place to go in the Hawaiian Islands is somewhere on Maui or Kauai or Hawaii has by now filtered down to such wide acceptance that one can only suspect Honolulu to be due for a revival.) Or, if they are of a more visionary turn, they talk, in a kind of James Michener rhetoric, about how Hawaii is a multiracial paradise and a labor-management paradise and a progressive paradise in which the past is now reconciled with the future, where the I.L.W.U.'s Jack Hall lunches at the Pacific Club and where that repository of everything old-line in Hawaii, the Bishop Estate, works hand in hand with Henry Kaiser to transform Koko Head into a $350 million development named Hawaii Kai. If they are in the travel business they talk about The Million Visitor Year (1970) and The Two Million Visitor Year (1980) and twenty thousand Rotarians convening in Honolulu in 1969 and they talk about The Product. "The reports show what we need," one travel man told me. "We need more attention to shaping and molding the product." The product is the place they live.

If they are from Honolulu but a little *arriviste*—say if they have been here only thirty years—they drop the name "Lowell" and talk about their charity work. If they are from Honolulu but not at all *arriviste* they talk about opening boutiques and going into the real-estate business and whether or not it was rude for Jacqueline Kennedy to appear for dinner at Henry Kaiser's in a muumuu and bare feet. ("I mean I *know* people come here to relax and not get dressed up, but still. . . .") They get to the mainland quite often but not often enough to be well-informed about what is going on there. They like to entertain and to be entertained and to have people coming through. ("What would it be like without them?" one woman asked me rhetorically. "It'd be Saturday night at the club in Racine, Wisconsin.") They are very gracious and very enthusiastic, and give such an appearance of health and happiness and hope that I sometimes find it difficult to talk to them. I think that they would not understand why I came to Hawaii, and I think that they will perhaps not understand what I am going to remember

1966

Rock of Ages

ALCATRAZ ISLAND is covered with flowers now: orange and yellow nasturtiums, geraniums, sweet grass, blue iris, black-eyed Susans. Candytuft springs up through the cracked concrete in the exercise yard. Ice plant carpets the rusting catwalks. "WARNING! KEEP OFF! U.S. PROPERTY," the sign still reads, big and yellow and visible for perhaps a quarter of a mile, but since March 21, 1963, the day they took the last thirty or so men off the island and sent them to prisons less expensive to maintain, the warning has been only *pro forma*, the gun turrets empty, the cell blocks abandoned. It is not an unpleasant place to be, out there on Alcatraz with only the flowers and the wind and a bell buoy moaning and the tide surging through the Golden Gate, but to like a place like that you have to want a moat.

I sometimes do, which is what I am talking about here. Three people live on Alcatraz Island now. John and Marie Hart live in the same apartment they had for the sixteen years that he was a prison guard; they raised five children on the island, back when their neighbors were the Birdman and Mickey Cohen, but the Birdman and Mickey Cohen are gone now and so are the Harts' children, moved away, the last married in a ceremony on the island in June 1966. One other person lives on Alcatraz, a retired merchant seaman named Bill Doherty, and, between them, John Hart and Bill Doherty are responsible to the General Services Administration for maintaining a twenty-four-hour watch over the twenty-two-acre island. John Hart has a dog named Duffy, and Bill Doherty has a dog named Duke, and although the dogs are primarily good company they are also the first line of defense on Alcatraz Island. Marie Hart has a corner window which looks out to the San Francisco skyline, across a mile and a half of bay, and she sits there and paints "views" or plays her organ, songs like "Old Black Joe" and "Please Go 'Way and Let Me Sleep." Once a week the Harts take their boat to San Francisco to pick up their mail and shop at the big Safeway in the Marina, and occasionally Marie Hart gets off the island to visit her children. She likes to keep in touch with them by telephone, but for ten months recently, after a Japanese freighter cut the cable, there was no telephone service to or from Alcatraz. Every morning the KGO traffic reporter drops the San Francisco *Chronicle* from his helicopter, and when he has time he stops for coffee. No one else comes out there except a man from the General Services Administration named Thomas Scott, who brings out an occasional congressman or somebody who wants to buy the island or, once in a while, his wife and small son, for a picnic. Quite a few people would like to buy the island, and Mr. Scott reckons that it would bring about five million dollars in a sealed-bid auction, but the General Services Administration is powerless to sell it until Congress acts on a standing proposal to turn the island into a "peace park." Mr. Scott says that he will be glad to get Alcatraz off his hands, but the charge of a fortress island could not be something a man gives up without ambivalent thoughts.

I went out there with him a while ago. Any child could imagine a prison more like a prison than Alcatraz looks, for what bars and wires there are seem perfunctory, beside the point; the island itself was the prison, and the cold tide its wall. It is precisely what they called it: the Rock. Bill Doherty and Duke lowered the dock for us, and in the station wagon on the way up the cliff Bill Doherty told Mr. Scott about small repairs he had made or planned to make. Whatever repairs get made on Alcatraz are made to pass the time, a kind of caretaker's scrimshaw, because the government pays for no upkeep at all on the prison; in 1963 it would have cost five million dollars to repair, which is why it was abandoned, and the $24,000 a year that it costs to maintain Alcatraz now is mostly for surveillance, partly to barge in the 400,000 gallons of water that Bill Doherty and the Harts use every year (there is no water at all on Alcatraz, one impediment to development), and the rest to heat two apartments and keep some lights burning. The buildings seem quite literally abandoned. The key locks have been ripped from the cell doors and the big electrical locking mechanisms disconnected. The tear-gas vents in the cafeteria are empty and the paint is buckling everywhere, corroded by the sea air, peeling off in great scales of pale green and ocher. I stood for a while in Al Capone's cell, five by nine feet, number 200 on the second tier of B Block, not one of the view cells, which were awarded on seniority, and I walked through the solitary block, totally black when the doors were closed. "Snail Mitchel," read a pencil scrawl on the wall of Solitary 14. "The only man that ever got shot for walking too slow." Beside it was a calendar, the months penciled on the wall with the days scratched off, May, June, July, August of some unnumbered year.

Mr. Scott, whose interest in penology dates from the day his office acquired Alcatraz as a potential property, talked about escapes and security routines and pointed out the beach where Ma Barker's son Doc was killed trying to escape. (They told him to come back up, and he said he would rather be shot, and he was.) I saw the shower room with the soap still in the dishes. I picked up a yellowed program from an Easter service (*Why seek ye the living among the dead? He is not here, but is risen*) and I struck a few notes on an upright piano with the ivory all rotted from the keys and I tried to imagine the prison as it had been, with the big lights playing over the windows all night long and the guards patrolling the gun galleries and the silverware clattering into a bag as it was checked in after meals, tried dutifully to summon up some distaste, some night terror of the doors locking and the boat pulling away. But the fact of it was that I liked it out there, a ruin devoid of human vanities, clean of human illusions, an empty place reclaimed by the weather where a woman plays an organ to stop the wind's whining and an old man plays ball with a dog named Duke. I could tell you that I came back because I had promises to keep, but maybe it was because nobody asked me to stay.

1967

The Seacoast of Despair

I WENT TO NEWPORT not long ago, to see
the great stone *fin-de-siècle* "cottages" in which
certain rich Americans once summered. The
places loom still along Bellevue Avenue and
Cliff Walk, one after another, silk curtains
frayed but gargoyles intact, monuments to
something beyond themselves; houses built,
clearly, to some transcendental point. No
one had made clear to me exactly what
that point was. I had been promised that
the great summer houses were museums
and warned that they were monstrosities,
had been assured that the way of life they
suggested was graceful beyond belief and
that it was gross beyond description, that
the very rich were different from you and
me and yes, they had lower taxes, and if
"The Breakers" was perhaps not entirely
tasteful, still, *où sont les croquet wickets d'an-
tan*. I had read Edith Wharton and I had
read Henry James, who thought that the

houses should stand there always, remind-
ers "of the peculiarly awkward vengeances
of affronted proportion and discretion."

But all that turns out to be beside the
point, all talk of taxes and taste and affronted
proportion. If, for example, one pursues the
course, as Mrs. Richard Gambrill did in
1900, of engaging the architect who did the
New York Public Library, approving plans
for an eighteenth-century French château on
a Rhode Island beach, ordering the garden
copied after one Henry VIII gave to Anne
Boleyn, and naming the result "Vernon
Court," one moves somehow beyond the
charge of breached "discretion." Something
else is at work here. No aesthetic judgment
could conceivably apply to the Newport of
Bellevue Avenue, to those vast follies behind
their hand-wrought gates; they are products
of the metastasis of capital, the Industrial
Revolution carried to its logical extreme, and
what they suggest is how recent are the notions that life should be "comfortable," that
those who live it should be "happy."

"Happiness" is, after all, a consumption
ethic, and Newport is the monument of a

society in which production was seen as the moral point, the reward if not exactly the end, of the economic process. The place is devoid of the pleasure principle. To have had the money to build "The Breakers" or "Marble House" or "Ochre Court" and to choose to build at Newport is in itself a denial of possibilities; the island is physically ugly, mean without the saving grace of extreme severity, a landscape less to be enjoyed than dominated. The prevalence of topiary gardening in Newport suggests the spirit of the place. And it was not as if there were no other options for these people: William Randolph Hearst built not at Newport but out on the edge of the Pacific. San Simeon, whatever its peculiarities, is in fact *la cuesta encantada*, swimming in golden light, sybaritic air, a deeply romantic place. But in Newport the air proclaims only the sources of money. Even as the sun dapples the great lawns and the fountains plash all around, there is something in the air that has nothing to do with pleasure and nothing to do with graceful tradition, a sense not of how prettily money can be spent but of how harshly money is made, an immediate presence of the pits and the rails and the foundries, of turbines and pork-belly futures. So insistent is the presence of money in Newport that the mind springs ineluctably to the raw beginnings of it. A contemplation of "Rosecliff" dissolves into the image of Big Jim Fair, digging the silver out of a mountain in Nevada so that his daughter might live in Newport. "Old Man Berwind, he'd turn in his grave to see that oil truck parked in the driveway," a guard at "The Elms" said to me as we surveyed the sunken garden there. "He made it in coal, soft coal." It had been on my mind as well as on the guard's, even as we stood in the sunlight outside the marble summer house, coal, soft coal, words like *bituminous* and *anthracite*, not the words of summer fancy.

In that way Newport is curiously Western, closer in spirit to Virginia City than to New York, to Denver than to Boston. It has the stridency usually credited to the frontier. And, like the frontier, it was not much of a game for women. Men paid for Newport, and granted to women the privilege of living in it. Just as gilt vitrines could be purchased for the correct display of biscuit Sèvres, so marble stairways could be bought for the advantageous display of women. In the filigreed gazebos they could be exhibited in a different light; in the French sitting rooms, in still another setting. They could be cajoled, flattered, indulged, given pretty rooms and Worth dresses, allowed to imagine that they ran their own houses and their own lives, but when it came time to negotiate, their freedom proved *trompe l'oeil*. It was the world of Bailey's Beach which made a neurasthenic of Edith Wharton, and, against her will, the Duchess of Marlborough of Consuelo Vanderbilt. The very houses are men's houses, factories, undermined by tunnels and service railways, shot through with plumbing to collect salt water, tanks to store it, devices to collect rain water, vaults for table silver, equipment inventories of china and crystal and "Tray cloths—fine" and "Tray cloths—ordinary." Somewhere in the bowels of "The Elms" is a coal bin twice the size of Julia Berwind's bedroom. The mechanics of such houses take precedence over all desires or inclinations; neither for great passions nor for morning whims can the factory be shut down, can production—of luncheons, of masked balls, of *marrons glacés*—be slowed. To stand in the dining room of "The Breakers" is to imagine fleeing from it, pleading migraine.

What Newport turns out to be, then, is homiletic, a fantastically elaborate stage setting for an American morality play in which money and happiness are presented as antithetical. It is a curious theatrical for these particular men to have conceived, but then we all judge ourselves sometime; it is hard for me to believe that Cornelius Vanderbilt did not sense, at some point in time, in some dim billiard room of his unconscious, that when he built "The Breakers" he damned himself. The world must have seemed greener to all of them, out there when they were young and began laying the rails or digging for high-grade ore in the Comstock or daring to think that they might corner copper. More than anyone else in the society, these men had apparently dreamed the dream and made it work. And what they did then was to build a place which seems to illustrate, as in a child's primer, that the production ethic led step by step to unhappiness, to restrictiveness, to entrapment in the mechanics of living. In that way the lesson of Bellevue Avenue is more seriously radical than the idea of Brook Farm. Who could fail to read the sermon in the stones of Newport? Who could think that the building of a railroad could guarantee salvation, when there on the lawns of the men who built the railroad nothing is left but the shadows of migrainous women, and the pony carts waiting for the long-dead children?

1967

Guaymas, Sonora

IT HAD RAINED in Los Angeles until the cliff was crumbling into the surf and I did not feel like getting dressed in the morning, so we decided to go to Mexico, to Guaymas, where it was hot. We did not go for marlin. We did not go to skin-dive. We went to get away from ourselves, and the way to do that is to drive, down through Nogales some day when the pretty green places pall and all that will move the imagination is some place difficult, some desert. The desert, any desert, is indeed the valley of the shadow of death; come back from the desert and you feel like Alcestis, reborn. After Nogales on Route 15 there is nothing but the Sonoran desert, nothing but mesquite and rattlesnakes and the Sierra Madre floating to the east, no trace of human endeavor but an occasional Pemex truck hurtling north and once in a while in the distance the dusty Pullman cars of the Ferrocarril del Pacífico.

Magdalena is on Route 15, and then Hermosillo, where the American ore and cattle buyers gather in the bar at the Hotel San Alberto. There is an airport in Hermosillo, and Hermosillo is only eighty-five miles above Guaymas, but to fly is to miss the point. The point is to become disoriented, shriven, by the heat and the deceptive perspectives and the oppressive sense of carrion. The road shimmers. The eyes want to close.

And then, just past that moment when the desert has become the only reality, Route 15 hits the coast and there is Guaymas, a lunar thrust of volcanic hills and islands with the warm Gulf of California lapping idly all around, lapping even at the cactus, the water glassy as a mirage, the ships in the harbor whistling unsettlingly, moaning, ghost schooners, landlocked, lost. That is Guaymas. As far as the town goes, Graham Greene might have written it: a shadowy square with a filigree pergola for the Sunday band, a racket of birds, a cathedral in bad repair with a robin's-egg-blue tile dome, a turkey buzzard on the cross. The wharves are piled with bales of Sonoran cotton and mounds of dark copper concentrates; out on the freighters with the Panamanian and Liberian flags the Greek and German boys stand in the hot twilight and stare sullenly at the grotesque and claustrophobic hills, at the still town, a curious limbo at which to call.

Had we really been intent upon losing ourselves we might have stayed in town, at a hotel where faded and broken turquoise-blue shutters open onto the courtyard, where old men sit in the doorways and nothing moves, but instead we stayed outside town, at the Playa de Cortés, the big old hotel built by the Southern Pacific before the railways were nationalized. That place was a mirage, too, lovely and cool with thick whitewashed walls and dark shutters and bright tiles, tables made from ebony railroad ties, pale appliqued muslin curtains, shocks of corn wrapped around the heavy beams. Pepper trees grew around the swimming pool, and lemons and bananas in the courtyard. The food was unremarkable, but after dinner one could lie in a hammock on the terrace and listen to the fountains and the sea. For a week we lay in hammocks and fished desultorily and went to bed early and got very brown and lazy. My husband caught eight sharks, and I read an oceanography textbook, and we did not talk much. At the end of the week we wanted to do something, but all there was to do was visit the tracking station for an old space program or go see John Wayne and Claudia Cardinale in *Circus World*, and we knew it was time to go home.

1965

Los Angeles Notebook

THERE IS SOMETHING UNEASY in the Los Angeles air this afternoon, some unnatural stillness, some tension. What it means is that tonight a Santa Ana will begin to blow, a hot wind from the northeast whining down through the Cajon and San Gorgonio Passes, blowing up sandstorms out along Route 66, drying the hills and the nerves to the flash point. For a few days now we will see smoke back in the canyons, and hear sirens in the night. I have neither heard nor read that a Santa Ana is due, but I know it, and almost everyone I have seen today knows it too. We know it because we feel it. The baby frets. The maid sulks. I rekindle a waning argument with the telephone company, then cut my losses and lie down, given over to whatever it is in the air. To live with the Santa Ana is to accept, consciously or unconsciously, a deeply mechanistic view of human behavior.

I recall being told, when I first moved to Los Angeles and was living on an isolated beach, that the Indians would throw themselves into the sea when the bad wind blew. I could see why. The Pacific turned ominously glossy during a Santa Ana period, and one woke in the night troubled not only by the peacocks screaming in the olive trees but by the eerie absence of surf. The heat was surreal. The sky had a yellow cast, the kind of light sometimes called "earthquake weather." My only neighbor would not come out of her house for days, and there were no lights at night, and her husband roamed the place with a machete. One day he would tell me that he had heard a trespasser, the next a rattlesnake.

"On nights like that," Raymond Chandler once wrote about the Santa Ana, "every booze party ends in a fight. Meek little wives feel the edge of the carving knife and study their husbands' necks. Anything can happen." That was the kind of wind it was. I did not know then that there was any basis for the effect it had on all of us, but it turns out to be another of those cases in which science bears out folk wisdom. The Santa Ana, which is named for one of the canyons it rushes through, is a *foehn* wind, like the *foehn* of Austria and Switzerland and the *hamsin* of Israel. There are a number of persistent malevolent winds, perhaps the best known of which are the mistral of France and the Mediterranean sirocco, but a *foehn* wind has distinct characteristics: it occurs on the leeward slope of a mountain range and, although the air begins as a cold mass, it is warmed as it comes down the mountain and appears finally as a hot dry wind. Whenever and wherever a *foehn* blows, doctors hear about headaches and nausea and allergies, about "nervousness," about "depression." In Los Angeles some teachers do not attempt to conduct formal classes during a Santa Ana, because the children become unmanageable. In Switzerland the suicide rate goes up during the *foehn*, and in the courts of some Swiss cantons the wind is considered a mitigating circumstance for crime. Surgeons are said to watch the wind, because blood does not clot normally during a *foehn*. A few years ago an

Israeli physicist discovered that not only during such winds, but for the ten or twelve hours which precede them, the air carries an unusually high ratio of positive to negative ions. No one seems to know exactly why that should be; some talk about friction and others suggest solar disturbances. In any case the positive ions are there, and what an excess of positive ions does, in the simplest terms, is make people unhappy. One cannot get much more mechanistic than that.

Easterners commonly complain that there is no "weather" at all in Southern California, that the days and the seasons slip by relentlessly, numbingly bland. That is quite misleading. In fact the climate is characterized by infrequent but violent extremes: two periods of torrential subtropical rains which continue for weeks and wash out the hills and send subdivisions sliding toward the sea; about twenty scattered days a year of the Santa Ana, which, with its incendiary dryness, invariably means fire. At the first prediction of a Santa Ana, the Forest Service flies men and equipment from northern California into the southern for-

ests, and the Los Angeles Fire Department
cancels its ordinary non-firefighting routines. The Santa Ana caused Malibu to
burn the way it did in 1956, and Bel Air in
1961, and Santa Barbara in 1964. In the
winter of 1966–67 eleven men were killed
fighting a Santa Ana fire that spread through
the San Gabriel Mountains.

Just to watch the front-page news out of
Los Angeles during a Santa Ana is to get
very close to what it is about the place. The
longest single Santa Ana period in recent
years was in 1957, and it lasted not the usual
three or four days but fourteen days, from
November 21 until December 4. On the
first day 25,000 acres of the San Gabriel
Mountains were burning, with gusts reaching 100 miles an hour. In town, the wind
reached Force 12, or hurricane force, on the
Beaufort Scale; oil derricks were toppled
and people ordered off the downtown
streets to avoid injury from flying objects.
On November 22 the fire in the San Gabri-
els was out of control. On November 24 six
people were killed in automobile accidents,
and by the end of the week the Los Angeles

Times was keeping a box score of traffic deaths. On November 26 a prominent Pasadena attorney, depressed about money, shot and killed his wife, their two sons, and himself. On November 27 a South Gate divorcée, twenty-two, was murdered and thrown from a moving car. On November 30 the San Gabriel fire was still out of control, and the wind in town was blowing eighty miles an hour. On the first day of December four people died violently, and on the third the wind began to break.

It is hard for people who have not lived in Los Angeles to realize how radically the Santa Ana figures in the local imagination. The city burning is Los Angeles's deepest image of itself: Nathanael West perceived that, in *The Day of the Locust*; and at the time of the 1965 Watts riots what struck the imagination most indelibly were the fires. For days one could drive the Harbor Freeway and see the city on fire, just as we had always known it would be in the end. Los Angeles weather is the weather of catastrophe, of apocalypse, and, just as the reliably long and bitter winters of New England determine the way life is lived there, so the violence and the unpredictability of the Santa Ana affect the entire quality of life in Los Angeles, accentuate its impermanence, its unreliability. The wind shows us how close to the edge we are.

2

"Here's why I'm on the beeper, Ron," said the telephone voice on the all-night radio show. "I just want to say that this *Sex for the Secretary* creature—whatever her name is— certainly isn't contributing anything to the morals in this country. It's pathetic. Statistics *show*."

"It's *Sex and the Office*, honey," the disc jockey said. "That's the title. By Helen Gurley Brown. Statistics show what?"

"I haven't got them right here at my fingertips, naturally. But they *show*."

"I'd be interested in hearing them. Be constructive, you Night Owls."

"All right, let's take *one* statistic," the voice said, truculent now. "Maybe I haven't read the book, but what's this business she recommends about *going out with married men for lunch?*"

So it went, from midnight until 5 a.m., interrupted by records and by occasional calls debating whether or not a rattlesnake can swim. Misinformation about rattlesnakes is a leitmotiv of the insomniac imagination in Los Angeles. Toward 2 a.m. a man from "out Tarzana way" called to protest. "The Night Owls who called earlier must have been thinking about, uh, *The Man in the Gray Flannel Suit* or some other book," he said, "because Helen's one of the few authors trying to tell us what's really going *on*. Hefner's another, and he's also controversial, working in, uh, another area."

An old man, after testifying that he "personally" had seen a swimming rattlesnake, in the Delta-Mendota Canal, urged "moderation" on the Helen Gurley Brown question. "We shouldn't get on the beeper to call things pornographic before we've read them," he complained, pronouncing it pornee-oh-graphic. "I say, get the book. Give it a chance." The original *provocateur* called back to agree that she would get the book. "And then I'll burn it," she added.

"Book burner, eh?" laughed the disc jockey good-naturedly.

"I wish they still burned witches," she hissed.

3

It is three o'clock on a Sunday afternoon and 105° and the air so thick with smog that the dusty palm trees loom up with a sudden and rather attractive mystery. I have been playing in the sprinklers with the baby and I get in the car and go to Ralph's Market on the corner of Sunset and Fuller wearing an old bikini bathing suit. That is not a very good thing to wear to the market but neither is it, at Ralph's on the corner of Sunset and Fuller, an unusual costume. Nonetheless a large woman in a cotton muumuu jams her cart into mine at the butcher counter. *"What a thing to wear to the market,"* she says in a loud but strangled voice. Everyone looks the other way and I study a plastic package of rib lamb chops and she repeats it. She follows me all over the store, to the Junior Foods, to the Dairy Products, to the Mexican Delicacies, jamming my cart whenever she can. Her husband plucks at her sleeve. As I leave the check-out counter she raises her voice one last time: "*What a thing to wear to Ralph's*," she says.

4

A party at someone's house in Beverly Hills: a pink tent, two orchestras, a couple of French Communist directors in Cardin evening jackets, chili and hamburgers from Chasen's. The wife of an English actor sits at a table alone; she visits California rarely although her husband works here a good deal. An American who knows her slightly comes over to the table.

"Marvelous to see you here," he says.

"Is it," she says.

"How long have you been here?"

"Too long."

She takes a fresh drink from a passing

waiter and smiles at her husband, who is dancing.

The American tries again. He mentions her husband.

"I hear he's marvelous in this picture."

She looks at the American for the first time. When she finally speaks she enunciates every word very clearly. "He . . . is . . . also . . . a . . . fag," she says pleasantly.

5

The oral history of Los Angeles is written in piano bars. "Moon River," the piano player always plays, and "Mountain Greenery." "There's a Small Hotel" and "This Is Not the First Time." People talk to each other, tell each other about their first wives and last husbands. "Stay funny," they tell each other, and "This is to die over." A construction man talks to an unemployed screenwriter who is celebrating, alone, his tenth wedding anniversary. The construction man is on a job in Montecito: "Up in Montecito," he says, "they got one square mile with 135 millionaires."

"Putrescence," the writer says.

"That's all you got to say about it?"

"Don't read me wrong, I think Santa Barbara's one of the most—Christ, *the* most—beautiful places in the world, but it's a beautiful place that contains a . . . *putrescence.* They just live on their putrescent millions."

"So give me putrescent."

"No, no," the writer says. "I just happen to think millionaires have some sort of lacking in their . . . in their elasticity."

A drunk requests "The Sweetheart of Sigma Chi." The piano player says he doesn't know it. "Where'd you learn to play the piano?" the drunk asks. "I got two degrees," the piano player says. "One in musical education." I go to a coin telephone and call a friend in New York. "Where are you?" he says. "In a piano bar in Encino," I say. "Why?" he says. "Why not," I say.

1965–67

Goodbye to All That

How many miles to Babylon?
Three score miles and ten—
Can I get there by candlelight?
Yes, and back again—
If your feet are nimble and light
You can get there by candlelight.

IT IS EASY to see the beginnings of things, and harder to see the ends. I can remember now, with a clarity that makes the nerves in the back of my neck constrict, when New York began for me, but I cannot lay my finger upon the moment it ended, can never cut through the ambiguities and second starts and broken resolves to the exact place on the page where the heroine is no longer as optimistic as she once was. When I first saw New York I was twenty, and it was summertime, and I got off a DC-7 at the old Idlewild temporary terminal in a new dress which had seemed very smart in Sacramento but seemed less smart already, even in the old Idlewild temporary terminal, and the warm air smelled of mildew and some instinct, programmed by all the movies I had ever seen and all the songs I had ever heard sung and all the stories I had ever read about New York, informed me that it would never be quite the same again. In fact it never was. Some time later there was a song on all the jukeboxes on the upper East Side that went "but where is the schoolgirl who used to be me," and if it was late enough at night I used to wonder that. I know now that almost everyone wonders something like that, sooner or later and no matter what he or she is doing, but one of the mixed blessings of being twenty and twenty-one and even twenty-three is the conviction that nothing like this, all evidence to the contrary notwithstanding, has ever happened to anyone before.

Of course it might have been some other city, had circumstances been different and the time been different and had I been different, might have been Paris or Chicago or even San Francisco, but because I am talking about myself I am talking here about New York. That first night I opened my window on the bus into town and watched for the skyline, but all I could see were the wastes of Queens and the big signs that said MIDTOWN TUNNEL THIS LANE and then a flood of summer rain (even that seemed remarkable and exotic, for I had come out of the West where there was no summer rain), and for the next three days I sat wrapped in blankets in a hotel room air-conditioned to 35° and tried to get over a bad cold and a high fever. It did not occur to me to call a doctor, because I knew none, and although it did occur to me to call the desk and ask that the air conditioner be turned off, I never called, because I did not know how much to tip whoever might come—was anyone ever so young? I am here to tell you that someone was. All I could do during those three days was talk long-distance to the boy I already knew I would never marry in the spring. I would stay in New York, I told him, just six months, and I could see the Brooklyn Bridge from my window. As it turned out the bridge was the Triborough, and I stayed eight years.

In retrospect it seems to me that those days before I knew the names of all the bridges were happier than the ones that came later, but perhaps you will see that as we go along. Part of what I want to tell you is what it is like to be young in New York, how six months can become eight years with the deceptive ease of a film dissolve, for that is how those years appear to me now, in a long sequence of sentimental dissolves and old-fashioned trick shots—the Seagram Building fountains dissolve into snowflakes, I enter a revolving door at twenty and come out a good deal older, and on a different street. But most particularly I want to explain to you, and in the process perhaps to myself, why I no longer live in New York. It is often said that New York is a city for only the very rich and the very poor. It is less often said that New York is also, at least for those of us who came there from somewhere else, a city for only the very young.

I remember once, one cold bright December evening in New York, suggesting to a friend who complained of having been around too long that he come with me to a party where there would be, I assured him with the bright resourcefulness of twenty-three, "new faces." He laughed literally until he choked, and I had to roll down the taxi window and hit him on the back. "New faces," he said finally, "don't tell me about *new faces*." It seemed that the last time he had gone to a party where he had been promised "new faces," there had been fifteen people in the room, and he had already slept with five of the women and owed money to all but two of the men. I laughed with him, but the first snow had just begun to fall and the big Christmas trees glittered yellow and white as far as I could see up Park Avenue and I had a new dress and it would be a long while before I would come to understand the particular moral of the story.

It would be a long while because, quite

simply, I was in love with New York. I do not mean "love" in any colloquial way, I mean that I was in love with the city, the way you love the first person who ever touches you and never love anyone quite that way again. I remember walking across Sixty-second Street one twilight that first spring, or the second spring, they were all alike for a while. I was late to meet someone but I stopped at Lexington Avenue and bought a peach and stood on the corner eating it and knew that I had come out of the West and reached the mirage. I could taste the peach and feel the soft air blowing from a subway grating on my legs and I could smell lilac and garbage and expensive perfume and I knew that it would cost something sooner or later—because I did not belong there, did not come from there—but when you are twenty-two or twenty-three, you figure that later you will have a high emotional balance, and be able to pay whatever it costs. I still believed in possibilities then, still had the sense, so peculiar to New York, that something extraordinary would happen any minute, any day, any month. I was making only $65 or $70 a week then ("Put yourself in Hattie Carnegie's hands," I was advised without the slightest trace of irony by an editor of the magazine for which I worked), so little money that some weeks I had to charge food at Bloomingdale's gourmet shop in order to eat, a fact which went unmentioned in the letters I wrote to California. I never told my father that I needed money because then he would have sent it, and I would never know if I could do it by myself. At that time making a living seemed a game to me, with arbitrary but quite inflexible rules. And except on a certain kind of winter evening—six-thirty in the Seventies, say, already dark and bitter with a wind off the river, when I would be walking very fast toward a bus and would look in the bright windows of brownstones and see cooks working in clean kitchens and imagine women lighting candles on the floor above and beautiful children being bathed on the floor above that—except on nights like those, I never felt poor; I had the feeling that if I needed money I could always get it. I could write a syndicated column for teenagers under the name "Debbi Lynn" or I could smuggle gold into India or I could become a $100 call girl, and none of it would matter.

Nothing was irrevocable; everything was within reach. Just around every corner lay something curious and interesting, something I had never before seen or done or known about. I could go to a party and meet someone who called himself Mr. Emotional Appeal and ran The Emotional Appeal Institute or Tina Onassis Blandford or a Florida cracker who was then a regular on what he called "the Big C," the Southampton-El Morocco circuit ("I'm well-connected on the Big C, honey," he would tell me over collard greens on his vast borrowed terrace), or the widow of the celery king of the Harlem market or a piano salesman from Bonne Terre, Missouri, or someone who had already made and lost two fortunes in Midland, Texas. I could make promises to myself and to other people and there would be all the time in the world to keep them. I could stay up all night and make mistakes, and none of it would count.

You see I was in a curious position in New York: it never occurred to me that I was living a real life there. In my imagination I was always there for just another few months, just until Christmas or Easter or the first warm day in May. For that reason I was most comfortable in the company of Southerners. They seemed to be in New York as I was, on some indefinitely extended leave from wherever they belonged, disinclined to consider the future, temporary exiles who always knew when the flights left for New Orleans or Memphis or Richmond or, in my case, California. Someone who lives always with a plane schedule in the drawer lives on a slightly different calendar. Christmas, for example, was a difficult season. Other people could take it in stride, going to Stowe or going abroad or going for the day to their mothers' places in Connecticut; those of us who believed that we lived somewhere else would spend it making and canceling airline reservations, waiting for weatherbound flights as if for the last plane out of Lisbon in 1940, and finally comforting one another, those of us who were left, with the oranges and mementos and smoked-oyster stuffings of childhood, gathering close, colonials in a far country.

Which is precisely what we were. I am not sure that it is possible for anyone brought up in the East to appreciate entirely what New York, the idea of New York, means to those of us who came out of the West and the South. To an Eastern child, particularly a child who has always had an uncle on Wall Street and who has spent several hundred Saturdays first at F. A. O. Schwarz and being fitted for shoes at Best's and then waiting under the Biltmore clock and dancing to Lester Lanin, New York is just a city, albeit *the* city, a plausible place for people to live. But to those of us who came from places where no one had heard of Lester Lanin and Grand Central Station was a Saturday radio program, where Wall Street and Fifth Avenue and Madison Avenue were not places at all but abstractions ("Money," and "High Fashion," and "The Hucksters"), New York was no mere city. It was instead an infinitely romantic notion, the mysterious nexus of all love and money and power, the shining and perishable dream itself. To think of "living" there was to reduce the miraculous to the mundane; one does not "live" at Xanadu.

In fact it was difficult in the extreme for me to understand those young women for whom New York was not simply an ephemeral Estoril but a real place, girls who bought toasters and installed new cabinets in their apartments and committed themselves to some reasonable future. I never bought any furniture in New York. For a year or so I lived in other people's apartments; after that I lived in the Nineties in an apartment furnished entirely with things taken from storage by a friend whose wife had moved away. And when I left the apartment in the Nineties (that was when I was leaving everything, when it was all breaking up) I left everything in it, even my winter clothes and the map of Sacramento County I had hung on the bedroom wall to remind me who I was, and I moved into a monastic four-room floor-through on Seventy-fifth Street. "Monastic" is perhaps misleading here, implying some chic severity; until after

I was married and my husband moved some furniture in, there was nothing at all in those four rooms except a cheap double mattress and box springs, ordered by telephone the day I decided to move, and two French garden chairs lent me by a friend who imported them. (It strikes me now that the people I knew in New York all had curious and self-defeating sidelines. They imported garden chairs which did not sell very well at Hammacher Schlemmer or they tried to market hair straighteners in Harlem or they ghosted exposés of Murder Incorporated for Sunday supplements. I think that perhaps none of us was very serious, *engagé* only about our most private lives.)

All I ever did to that apartment was hang fifty yards of yellow theatrical silk across the bedroom windows, because I had some idea that the gold light would make me feel better, but I did not bother to weight the curtains correctly and all that summer the long panels of transparent golden silk would blow out the windows and get tangled and drenched in the afternoon thunderstorms. That was the year, my twenty-eighth, when

I was discovering that not all of the promises would be kept, that some things are in fact irrevocable and that it had counted after all, every evasion and every procrastination, every mistake, every word, all of it.

That is what it was all about, wasn't it? Promises? Now when New York comes back to me it comes in hallucinatory flashes, so clinically detailed that I sometimes wish that memory would effect the distortion with which it is commonly credited. For a lot of the time I was in New York I used a perfume called *Fleurs de Rocaille*, and then *L'Air du Temps*, and now the slightest trace of either can short-circuit my connections for the rest of the day. Nor can I smell Henri Bendel jasmine soap without falling back into the past, or the particular mixture of spices used for boiling crabs. There were barrels of crab boil in a Czech place in the Eighties where I once shopped. Smells, of course, are notorious memory stimuli, but there are other things which affect me the

same way. Blue-and-white striped sheets.
Vermouth cassis. Some faded nightgowns
which were new in 1959 or 1960, and some
chiffon scarves I bought about the same
time.

I suppose that a lot of us who have been
young in New York have the same scenes on
our home screens. I remember sitting in a
lot of apartments with a slight headache
about five o'clock in the morning. I had a
friend who could not sleep, and he knew a
few other people who had the same trouble,
and we would watch the sky lighten and
have a last drink with no ice and then go
home in the early morning light, when the
streets were clean and wet (had it rained in
the night? we never knew) and the few cruis-
ing taxis still had their headlights on and
the only color was the red and green of traffic signals. The White Rose bars opened
very early in the morning; I recall waiting in
one of them to watch an astronaut go into
space, waiting so long that at the moment
it actually happened I had my eyes not on
the television screen but on a cockroach
on the tile floor. I liked the bleak branches

above Washington Square at dawn, and the monochromatic flatness of Second Avenue, the fire escapes and the grilled storefronts peculiar and empty in their perspective.

It is relatively hard to fight at six-thirty or seven in the morning without any sleep, which was perhaps one reason we stayed up all night, and it seemed to me a pleasant time of day. The windows were shuttered in that apartment in the Nineties and I could sleep a few hours and then go to work. I could work then on two or three hours' sleep and a container of coffee from Chock Full O' Nuts. I liked going to work, liked the soothing and satisfactory rhythm of getting out a magazine, liked the orderly progression of four-color closings and two-color closings and black-and-white closings and then The Product, no abstraction but something which looked effortlessly glossy and could be picked up on a newsstand and weighed in the hand. I liked all the minutiae of proofs and layouts, liked working late on the nights the magazine went to press, sitting and reading *Variety* and waiting for the copy desk to call. From my office I could look across town to the weather signal on the Mutual of New York Building and the lights that alternately spelled out TIME and LIFE above Rockefeller Plaza; that pleased me obscurely, and so did walking uptown in the mauve eight o'clocks of early summer evenings and looking at things, Lowestoft tureens in Fifty-seventh Street windows, people in evening clothes trying to get taxis, the trees just coming into full leaf, the lambent air, all the sweet promises of money and summer.

Some years passed, but I still did not lose that sense of wonder about New York. I began to cherish the loneliness of it, the sense that at any given time no one need know where I was or what I was doing. I liked walking, from the East River over to the Hudson and back on brisk days, down around the Village on warm days. A friend would leave me the key to her apartment in the West Village when she was out of town, and sometimes I would just move down there, because by that time the telephone was beginning to bother me (the canker, you see, was already in the rose) and

not many people had that number. I remember one day when someone who did
have the West Village number came to
pick me up for lunch there, and we both
had hangovers, and I cut my finger opening him a beer and burst into tears, and we
walked to a Spanish restaurant and drank
Bloody Marys and *gazpacho* until we felt
better. I was not then guilt-ridden about
spending afternoons that way, because I
still had all the afternoons in the world.

And even that late in the game I still
liked going to parties, all parties, bad parties, Saturday-afternoon parties given by
recently married couples who lived in
Stuyvesant Town, West Side parties given
by unpublished or failed writers who served
cheap red wine and talked about going to
Guadalajara, Village parties where all the
guests worked for advertising agencies and
voted for Reform Democrats, press parties
at Sardi's, the worst kinds of parties. You
will have perceived by now that I was not
one to profit by the experience of others,
that it was a very long time indeed before I
stopped believing in new faces and began to

understand the lesson in that story, which was that it is distinctly possible to stay too long at the Fair.

I could not tell you when I began to understand that. All I know is that it was very bad when I was twenty-eight. Everything that was said to me I seemed to have heard before, and I could no longer listen. I could no longer sit in little bars near Grand Central and listen to someone complaining of his wife's inability to cope with the help while he missed another train to Connecticut. I no longer had any interest in hearing about the advances other people had received from their publishers, about plays which were having second-act trouble in Philadelphia, or about people I would like very much if only I would come out and meet them. I had already met them, always. There were certain parts of the city which I had to avoid. I could not bear upper Madison Avenue on weekday mornings (this was a particularly inconvenient aversion, since I then lived just fifty or sixty feet east of Madison), because I would see women walking Yorkshire terriers and shopping at Gristede's, and some Veblenesque gorge would rise in my throat. I could not go to Times Square in the afternoon, or to the New York Public Library for any reason whatsoever. One day I could not go into a Schrafft's; the next day it would be Bonwit Teller.

I hurt the people I cared about, and insulted those I did not. I cut myself off from the one person who was closer to me than any other. I cried until I was not even aware when I was crying and when I was not, cried in elevators and in taxis and in Chinese laundries, and when I went to the doctor he said only that I seemed to be depressed, and should see a "specialist." He wrote down a psychiatrist's name and address for me, but I did not go.

Instead I got married, which as it turned out was a very good thing to do but badly timed, since I still could not walk on upper Madison Avenue in the mornings and still could not talk to people and still cried in Chinese laundries. I had never before understood what "despair" meant, and I am not sure that I understand now, but I understood that year. Of course I could not work. I could not even get dinner with any degree of certainty, and I would sit in the apartment on Seventy-fifth Street paralyzed until my husband would call from his office and say gently that I did not have to get dinner, that I could meet him at Michael's Pub or at Toots Shor's or at Sardi's East. And then one morning in April (we had been married in January) he called and told me that he wanted to get out of New York for a while, that he would take a six-month leave of absence, that we would go somewhere.

It was three years ago that he told me that, and we have lived in Los Angeles since. Many of the people we knew in New York think this a curious aberration, and in fact tell us so. There is no possible, no adequate answer to that, and so we give certain stock answers, the answers everyone gives. I talk about how difficult it would be for us to "afford" to live in New York right now, about how much "space" we need. All I mean is that I was very young in New York, and that

at some point the golden rhythm was broken, and I am not that young any more. The
last time I was in New York was in a cold
January, and everyone was ill and tired.
Many of the people I used to know there
had moved to Dallas or had gone on Ant-
abuse or had bought a farm in New Hamp-
shire. We stayed ten days, and then we took
an afternoon flight back to Los Angeles, and
on the way home from the airport that night
I could see the moon on the Pacific and
smell jasmine all around and we both knew
that there was no longer any point in keeping the apartment we still kept in New York.
There were years when I called Los Angeles
"the Coast," but they seem a long time ago.

1967

ACKNOWLEDGMENTS

"Where the Kissing Never Stops" appeared first in *The New York Times Magazine* under the title "Just Folks at a School for Non-Violence." "On Keeping a Notebook" and "Notes from a Native Daughter" appeared first in *Holiday*. "I Can't Get That Monster out of My Mind" and "On Morality" first appeared in *The American Scholar*, the latter under the title "The Insidious Ethic of Conscience." "On Self-Respect" and "Guaymas, Sonora" appeared first in *Vogue*. "Los Angeles Notebook" includes a section which was published as "The Santa Ana" in *The Saturday Evening Post*. All the other essays appeared originally in *The Saturday Evening Post*, several under different titles: "Some Dreamers of the Golden Dream" was published as "How Can I Tell Them There's Nothing Left"; "7000 Romaine, Los Angeles 38," was published as "The Howard Hughes Underground";

"Letter from Paradise, 21° 19′N., 157° 52′W." was called "Hawaii: Taps Over Pearl Harbor"; "Goodbye to All That" was called "Farewell to the Enchanted City."

The author is grateful to all these publications for permission to reprint the various essays.